What Your Colleagues Are Saying . . .

Every educator is struggling with supporting ELs in a systemic, sustainable way. This book simplifies what's necessary while advocating for a sense of urgency to review data, assess models, and support EL teachers in utilizing best practices and ongoing professional learning.

Dana Salles Trevethan
Superintendent
Turlock Unified School District, CA

This book provides campus and district leadership with clearly defined reasons for supporting an equitable campus program for all learners, especially ELs. The scenarios and guiding questions are useful in initiating relevant discussion and provoking thoughtful discussions. Ayanna Cooper writes in a manner that will enhance EL advocacy for leaders regardless of EL experience.

Joseph Cerna
Elementary Principal and Adjunct Professor of Educational Leadership
Fort Sam Houston Elementary and Texas A&M San Antonio

A great resource for school leaders and English language directors. This book is a complete resource to assist with launching or enhancing an English language program in any school.

Laura Schaffer Metcalfe
Education Faculty
Grand Canyon University, AZ

This book is a practical and useful tool for building administrators and all who are interested in assessing their current models for supporting EL learners with an eye to improving their programs. It's practical and easy to read with great suggestions that you can use and implement immediately.

Marianne Lucas Lescher
School Principal
Kyrene Traditional Academy, AZ

This book highlights the importance of administrators developing the skills, supports, and structures that support English learners in achieving academic success and strengthening wellbeing. Cooper presents an array of considerations for administrators including: reflecting on personal knowledge, identifying areas for personal learning, building staff capacity and recognizing this must be through a job-embedded model, staffing, targeting instruction to reduce linguistic gaps for learners, and working to support parents with information and collaborating as partners.

Maryam Hasan
Vice Principal
Toronto District School Board, Toronto, Canada

This book offers a compelling message of hope for our linguistically diverse learners. An easy read for busy educators and a resource for administrators. This is the one tool needed that is research based and proven to enhance the professional learning model of one's organization to support student achievement.

Debra Paradowski
Associate Principal
Arrowhead Union High School, WI

This is an easy-to-read and easy-to-implement book. Each chapter is carefully broken down. Educators will find a lot of useful ideas within each chapter. The questions that are posed as a way of taking inventory of what you are currently doing in your school are extremely helpful and easy to use.

Lindsay Morhart
Teacher
Regina Catholic School Division, Saskatchewan, Canada

And Justice for ELs is an excellent guide for practitioners who seek to provide their English learners with high quality instruction in all subject areas. Too often such students are relegated an education that marginalizes them academically and fails to develop their native language skills. We can and must do a better job for these students and in this book Ayanna Cooper shows us how. Written in a clear and straightforward manner, this book will be an invaluable resource for educators who seek to make a difference.

Pedro A. Noguera
Distinguished Professor of Education Faculty and
Director of the Center for the Transformation of Schools
UCLA Graduate School of Education & Information Studies

School leaders will appreciate that Dr. Cooper's text takes them beyond legal compliance and moves their school toward real equity, excellence, and meaningful engagement for their English learners. Her essential questions will promote action-focused conversations that move the needle significantly toward justice and excellence for all.

Tim Boals
WIDA Founder and Director

Dr. Ayanna Cooper has made an incredible contribution to the field of education. And Justice For ELs equips educational leaders with the knowledge and confidence to create sustainable change as schools across the United States strive to meet the unique needs of English learners.

Sharon H. Porter, EdD
Executive Director
Next In Line to Lead Aspiring Principal Leadership Academy

Dr. Ayanna Cooper's And Justice for ELs is a must-read for school leaders and other educators who wish to move their schools and districts from equity to excellence in order to fully serve their ELs. Framed in research, law, and policy, yet rooted in practical actions, this book will provide a clear path to educators who desire to do what's right and just for their students and families.

Diane Staehr Fenner
Author of "Unlocking Englisher Learners' Potential"
and President of SupportEd Consulting

And Justice for ELs

A Leader's Guide to Creating and Sustaining Equitable Schools

Ayanna Cooper

Foreword by Margarita Espino Calderón

FOR INFORMATION:

Corwin

A SAGE Company

2455 Teller Road

Thousand Oaks, California 91320

(800) 233-9936

www.corwin.com

SAGE Publications Ltd.

1 Oliver's Yard

55 City Road

London, EC1Y 1SP

United Kingdom

SAGE Publications India Pvt. Ltd.

B 1/I 1 Mohan Cooperative Industrial Area

Mathura Road, New Delhi 110 044

India

SAGE Publications Asia-Pacific Pte. Ltd.

18 Cross Street #10-10/11/12

China Square Central

Singapore 048423

Program Director and Publisher: Dan Alpert

Senior Content Development Editor: Lucas Schleicher

Associate Content Development Editor: Mia Rodriguez

Production Editor: Megha Negi

Copy Editor: Integra

Typesetter: Hurix Digital

Proofreader: Rae-Ann Goodwin

Indexer: Integra

Cover Designer: Candice Harman

Graphic Designer: Candice Harman

Marketing Manager: Stephanie Trkay

Printed in the United States of America.

Library of Congress Cataloging-in-Publication Data

Names: Cooper, Ayanna, author.

Title: And justice for ELs : a leader's guide to creating and sustaining equitable schools / Ayanna Cooper.

Description: First edition. | Thousand Oaks, California : Corwin Press, Inc., [2021] | Includes bibliographical references.

Identifiers: LCCN 2020025110 | ISBN 9781544388144 (paperback) | ISBN 9781071822319 (epub) | ISBN 9781071822302 (epub) | ISBN 9781071822296 (ebook)

Subjects: LCSH: English language—Study and teaching—Foreign speakers.

Classification: LCC PE1128.A2 C6898 2020 | DDC 428.0071—dc23

LC record available at https://lccn.loc.gov/2020025110>

This book is printed on acid-free paper.

SUSTAINABLE FORESTRY INITIATIVE

Certified Chain of Custody
Promoting Sustainable Forestry
www.sfiprogram.org
SFI-01268

20 21 22 23 24 10 9 8 7 6 5 4 3 2 1

Table of Contents

Visit the companion website at
http://resources.corwin.com/justiceforels
for downloadable resources.

Foreword

Creating and Sustaining Equitable Schools with English Learners

Research published by the Wallace Foundation and others has shown that next to teaching, leadership is the school-related factor that most contributes to what students learn at school. Good principals serve as multipliers of effective teaching. Higher quality principals correlate to lower teacher turnover and increased teacher satisfaction, with greater impact in disadvantaged schools (2004).

As a parallel with the Wallace findings, the data about educational change and accountability in underserved EL communities paint a stark picture of the challenge facing schools today. The challenge for principals in schools with high multilingual/EL populations is not just about making good decisions, which is daunting enough. They must also manage often emotionally charged issues among faculty and community. The state of many of these schools calls for a dramatic shift in approach to EL achievement and school success. The shift must begin with a thorough understanding of the federal laws that protect the civil rights of ELs, then, build upon these to go from compliance to excellence (Calderón, 2012-19; Slakk & Calderón, 2020).

For the past ten years, I have worked with U.S.D.O.J. as an expert to help them identify issues that needed guidelines for coming into compliance. It was evident that they mostly lacked knowledge of ELs' civil rights laws. Even after the Dear Colleague letter (USDOJ/USDOE January 7, 2015) was sent to all school districts across the country, very few became familiar with the intent of its guidelines. Fewer could figure out where to start the necessary changes.

Fortunately, U.S. Secretary of Education Betsy DeVos recently announced that the Office for Civil Rights (OCR) at the U.S. Department of Education will launch the Outreach, Prevention, Education and Non-discrimination (OPEN) Center to focus on proactive compliance with federal civil rights laws. The OPEN Center will provide assistance and support to schools, educators, families, and students to ensure better awareness of the requirements and protections of federal non-discrimination laws. While they gear up, the field has this great book to start examining and moving toward creating and sustaining equitable schools with English Learners.

It was a pleasure reading this book that contains the basic information school principals need to support English learners. It goes through the 10 guidelines issued by the Dear Colleague letter in uncomplicated ways, offering many practical examples, scenarios and tools. The Dear Colleague letter also became the cornerstone of ESSA EL accountability. Therefore, it behooves all school leaders to become familiar with its contents and implications by discussing the chapters of this book.

The book begins with a whole chapter on student identification processes. The coverage of the cumbersome process of differentiating between proficiency levels and dually identified ELs/Special education ELs provides examples and ways to facilitate implementing this process. It touches on program models but Chapter 2 elaborates on the program models by differentiating models for special populations such as newcomers, elementary, middle and high schools. Dr. Cooper discusses approaches to scheduling in the high school to ensure that required services are offered. The chapter touches on other DOJ/DOE guidelines: staffing and staff development and parental engagement. Scenarios and checklists will help committees consider new ways of addressing compliance.

Bruce Joyce and Beverly Showers (2002) wrote about the importance of quality professional development that includes theory presentation, modeling, practice and feedback during a comprehensive initial training, followed by classroom coaching. In order to ensure transfer from training or any professional learning, collegial observations and feedback appear to have the most impact on teachers' instructional delivery and student learning. Their work has been replicated continuously with great effects. However, most schools spend their professional development funds on the trend-of-the-day workshop or send educators to conferences of their choice. Too often, there are no systematic plans for comprehensive whole-school learning, and funds for coaching, collegial planning, co-teaching planning, and lesson development are overlooked.

It was gratifying to read Chapter 4 because it discusses how a comprehensive professional learning plan can be developed beginning with a cycle of inquiry followed by a set of action steps. Dr. Cooper goes into specifics for preparing a needs assessment. Moreover, a set of questions, examples, and scenarios guides the reader in developing the learning plan. The chapter provides good suggestions to schools that are struggling with data. There are also examples for supporting teachers that include coaching, co-teaching, common planning time, and teacher self-assessments that lead to career-long practices. Dr. Cooper recommends some traditional professional development programs but also states that it is not a comprehensive list. Therefore, the process suggested for developing the school's learning plan promises to be more effective.

The final chapter lays out ways of reaching out to parents and sustaining their engagement. As with other chapters, it also spells out and dovetails with the requirement by DOJ-DOE. School engagement with parents of multilingual students, particularly non-English speaking parents, has been one of the most difficult challenges for schools. This chapter provides solid ideas for reaching out to parents.

Useful tools for planning or revamping a plan called "What would you do" and "Bringing it all together" appear at the end of each chapter. These sections summarize key ideas, followed by a set of questions for reflection. All in all, this is a great book for revisiting existing EL plans and making sure all are addressing compliance.

Margarita Espino Calderón
President/CEO, Margarita Calderón & Associates, Inc.
Professor Emerita, Senior Research Scientist
John Hopkins University, Graduate School of Education

REFERENCES ....

Calderón, M. E. (2012-2019). *Recommendations for the Massachusetts Department of Elementary and Secondary Education on the Delivery and Materials for Preparing Teachers and Administrators on Effective Instruction for ELLs: Reports to the United States Department of Justice.* Washington, DC: USDOJ.

U.S. Department of Justice & U.S. Department of Education (2015, January 7). Retrieved from https://www2.ed.gov/about/offices/list/ocr/letters/colleague-el-201501.pdf

Joyce, B., and Showers, B. (2002). Student achievement through staff development (3rd ed.). Alexandria, VA: Association for Supervision and Curriculum Development.

Leithwood, K. Louis, K.S., Anderson, A. & Wahlstrom, K. (2004). *Review of research: How leadership influences student learning.* New York, NY: The Wallace Foundation. Retrieved from https://www.wallacefoundation.org/knowledge-center/pages/a-review-of-research-how-leadership-influences-student-learning.aspx

Slakk, S., & Calderón, M. E. (2020). From compliance to excellence. In D. Alpert (Ed.), M. E. Calderón, M. G. Dove, D. S. Fennter, M. Gottlieb, A. Honigsfeld, T. W. Singer, . . . , D. Zacarian, *Breaking down the wall: Essential shifts for English learners' success* (pp. 21–45). Thousand Oaks, CA: Corwin Press.

Acknowledgments

Author's Acknowledgments

This book project started because of the leadership learning communities I have been so fortunate to be part of. Throughout this process, there have been a number of colleagues who have served as my peers, partners, critics, encouragers, motivators, and fellow advocates for traditionally marginalized students, specifically English learners. It is my hope that this book serves as evidence of the power of our synergy.

For those leaders who have been dedicated champions for the students and communities they serve, for allowing me to engage in the work alongside you, thank you for what you do each day for students. This list includes Kwame Asanti, Chris Bearden, Roy Dawson, Babatunji Ifarinu, Nadia Ramcharan, LaVern Shan, Naja Solomon, and Mark Willimas.

I'd also like to thank those who serve as teacher educators with a focus on culturally and linguistically diverse learners. Thank you for your dedication to preparing the next generation of teachers: Holly Arnold, Kisha Bryan, Elfrieda Lepp-Kaethler, Christine Leader, and Margo Williams. Thank you to those who support state, district, and school initiatives with a focus on equity, access, and high-quality standards-based instruction for all: Julie Carroll, Shelley Jallow, Kirsi Laine, Kiesha Lamb, Tiffany Alvarez-Smith, Cherrilynn Woods-Washington, Mayra Valtierrez, and Vanna White. I commend you all for the work you have committed to and for the work we have done together.

I especially appreciate those educators who contributed to this book by directly sharing their experiences through writing. Thank you to Asha Asby, Chanda Austin, Maria Rodriguez Burns, Phoenicia Grant, Norman Sauce, and Kimberly Skukalek. To Laura Gardner, for her guidance and contributions to Chapter 5, thank you for helping me to bring attention to these issues.

Thank you to the Corwin community, without whose support this book might never have come into existence. To Dan Alpert, who thoroughly listened to and welcomed my idea for this book: Many thanks to you for remaining dedicated to the causes of assuring equity, access and the civil rights of English learners. To the editorial staff Mia Rodriguez and Lucas Schleicher and my marketing manager, Maura Sullivan, thank you for supporting this work. To Megha Negi, my production editor, thank you for all your hard work. To Tomiko Breland, I cannot express my appreciation enough for your partnership and expertise as editor throughout the development of this book.

Finally, I'd like to express my sincere appreciation to my family members. To my nieces, the next generation of social justice advocates. Brandi Artez (for those lyrics) and Teneal Cooper for the engaging conversations (via text message). To my husband Ronnie, our children Ronnie and Breanna, my grandson Hendrix, and my mother Deborah for their ongoing support and unwavering belief that I could and would be successful in writing this book.

Publisher's Acknowledgments

Corwin gratefully acknowledges the contributions of the following reviewers:

Barbara Marler
Educational Administrator
Skokie School District 68 and National Louis University
Skokie, IL

Dana Salles Trevethan
Superintendent
Turlock Unified School District
Turlock, CA

Debra Paradowski
Associate Principal
Arrowhead Union High School
Hartland, WI

Jacie Maslyk
Assistant Superintendent
Hopewell Area School District
Aliquippa, PA

Joseph N. Cerna, EdD
Elementary Principal and Adjunct Professor Educational Leadership
Fort Sam Houston Elementary and Texas A&M San Antonio
Fort Sam Houston, TX

Laura Schaffer Metcalfe
Education Faculty
Grand Canyon University
Phoenix, AZ

Lindsay Morhart
Teacher
Regina Catholic School Division
Regina, Saskatchewan

Marianne Lucas Lescher, PhD
School Principal
Kyrene Traditional Academy
Chandler AZ

Maryam Hasan
Vice Principal
Toronto District School Board
Toronto, Ontario

About the Author

Ayanna Cooper, EdD, is a consultant, advocate for culturally and linguistically diverse learners, and a U.S. Department of State English Language Specialist alumna. As owner of A. Cooper Consulting, her projects involve providing technical assistance internationally and to state departments of education, school districts, and nonprofit organizations. She emphasizes the importance of building the capacity of district and school leaders to develop and manage English language programs and improve the instructional practices of teachers of English learners. She is a coauthor of *Evaluating ALL Teachers of English Learners and Students With Disabilities: Supporting Great Teaching* (with Staehr Fenner and Kozik) and coeditor of *Black Immigrants in the United States: Essays on the Politics of Race, Language, and Voice* (with Ibrahim). She has contributed to a number of books and publications, such as the WIDA *Essential Actions Handbook* and *Language Magazine*. She also writes a monthly blog focused on the civil rights of English learners for TESOL International Association. As a plenary speaker and frequent conference presenter, she has had the opportunity to share her work across the United States and internationally. In addition to teaching English as a second language, she has held a number of positions throughout her career, such as English learner instructional coach, urban education teacher supervisor, Title III director, and bilingual program specialist. Dr. Cooper is currently serving on the executive board of TESOL International Association.

Introduction

This book is a result of the numerous conversations, experiences, and frustrations I've had as an educator committed to culturally and linguistically diverse learners. Despite the number of initiatives focused on diverse student populations, specifically English learners (ELs), achievement gaps persist. From my experience, whether in the continental United States or abroad, the postal codes and climates may be different, but the challenges being faced by ELs and their learning communities are far too similar. The issues they confront are civil rights issues. I do not believe that educators wake up each morning with the intent of violating the civil rights of their students, but, unfortunately, it happens. It happens unintentionally yet regularly. Though we have made some strides by highlighting the rich cultural and linguistic diversity ELs possess, deficit mindset, anti-inclusive practices, racist rhetoric, and *pobrecito*, attitudes persist. Efforts to close the achievement gap are taking too long, despite all of our best efforts. Our students cannot wait any longer!

I approached writing this book as an ethnographer, using my field notes to explain and provide insight into a phenomenon I had witnessed time and time again. I've found that the fewest number of professional learning opportunities have been designed and facilitated specifically for the needs of school leaders who educate ELs. I was reminded recently that you don't have to be an expert to ask the right questions. This book is guided by a primary question: If educators are truly committed to equity and access for all, then why are certain subgroups of students, particularly ELs, still lagging behind?

This book is intended to serve as a conversation starter, one that poses a number of questions that are aimed at invoking critical thinking and self-reflection. The book is a form of social justice, activism, and response to the question of why ELs are being left behind. For school leaders, this book is particularly important because daily choices are made in schools that will have long-term implications, both positive and negative, for their ELs. It is my hope that this book serves as a resource and a new professional learning opportunity that will contribute to the construction of not one, but many bridges.

What This Book Is

In response to the plight of marginalized subgroups, many novice and experienced school leaders are looking for new approaches to the work. In response to that need, in just five chapters I address the civil rights mandates for ELs and how to best implement and sustain practices to support positive outcomes for students learning English as an additional language.

The chapters each get to the "heart of the matter" in a practical way—a way that does not exclude those without extensive backgrounds in English language teaching and learning. Because many such school leaders are already serving as advocates and leading schools with subgroups of ELs, this book is designed to welcome and invite them to the conversation. Each chapter includes one or more examples of situations that play out in schools on a daily basis that directly impact ELs and their families, a "What Would You Do" scenario, follow-up questions, and a list of related resources aimed at continuing these conversations. This book is a resource to help guide educators in learning about and leading schools with culturally and linguistically diverse learners in a way that assures linguistic equity.

What This Book Is Not

This book does not address all of the variables that contribute to the current state of EL achievement in the United States. It does not profess to have all of the answers. This book can support educators in examining their own contexts (rural, suburban, and urban) by encouraging them to make necessary improvements. It does not subscribe to a one-size-fits-all approach to creating and sustaining equitable schools. Each learning community is unique, with its own ecosystem of complexities and characteristics. Because it is impossible to provide specific advice or guidance for every possible situation, through this book's five chapters I have highlighted the "need-to-knows" necessary for school leaders to be able to make informed decisions about and for the ELs they serve.

How This Book Can Be Used

Warning: This book may be used to upset the status quo. This book may be used to challenge prior practices, systems, and structures. It can be used to inform individuals and learning communities who not only seek to deepen their understanding of EL needs and requirements but who want to be prepared to do what is necessary. This includes those who are influential in preservice educator programs, education policy, education reform, and the like. Cognitive dissonance laced with the spirit of activism can lead to more informed decision-making, collaborative partnerships, and, ultimately, the capacity to create and sustain equitable schools with ELs.

This book is dedicated to my parents, Deborah Wornum and the late Leonard Johnson, and to my stepfather, the late Bruce Wornum. It is also dedicated to my husband Ronnie and our children, Ronnie and Breanna Cooper, and my grandson Hendrix Cooper. Thank you for helping me to become the person I am today and will become in the future.

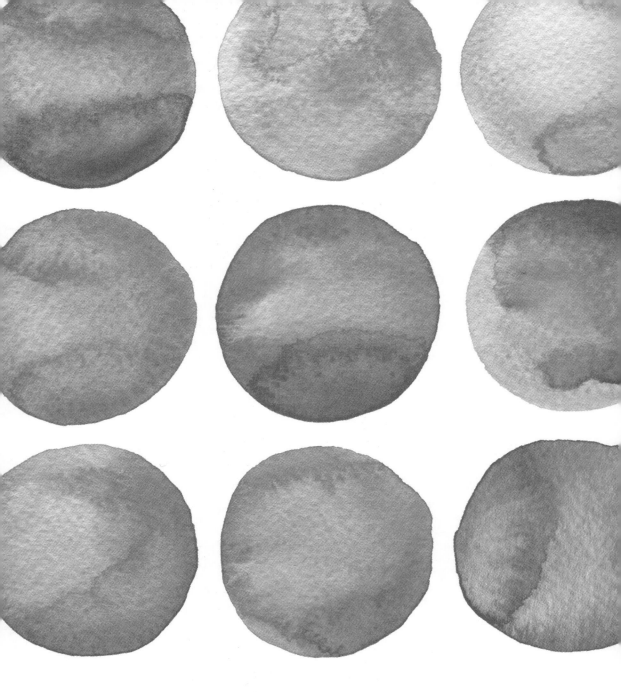

*Every student has the right to
a high quality, differentiated, standards-based,
culturally responsive education.*

English Learners in Your School and What You Need to Know and Do to Support Them

Are you an educator who supports students identified as English learners (ELs)? This book is designed to facilitate action-focused conversations among educators, linguistically diverse families, and stakeholders who want to do what's best, what is just, and what is required for the ELs they are responsible for. This book serves as a guide to help school leaders, and those who want to assure that ELs receive an equitable educational experience, to become linguistic equity advocates and catalysts for change by connecting the federal mandates to actionable steps needed to create and sustain equitable schools with ELs.

Although a number of books have been written for school leaders of ELs, this book provides a fresh perspective that is aligned to the civil rights mandates issued by the U.S. Department of Civil Rights, the U.S. Department of Justice, and the U.S. Department of Education Office of English Language Acquisition. This guidance is especially important for educators who are responsible for creating, sustaining, and managing highly effective learning communities for linguistically diverse learners. This book will help you move from awareness to action.

There are a number of asset-based terms and acronyms to describe students who are learning English as a new or additional language. Some of those acronyms include DLL (dual language learners), MLL (multilingual learners), and bilingual/biliterate students. For the sake of this text, in an effort to use the terminology currently used in federal guidance, the term *EL* is used.

Common Acronyms in English Language Teaching

DLL	Dual language learner
EL/ELL	English learner/English language learner
ELD	English language development
ELP	English language proficiency
ENL	English as a new language
ESOL	English to speakers of other languages
HLS	Home language survey
L1	First language or home language

L2	Second language
M1	Monitored Year 1, the first year after reaching proficiency
M2	Monitored Year 2, the second year after reaching proficiency
MLL	Multilingual learner
PHLOTE	Primary home language other than English
PL	Professional learning

Scenario: Awareness and Action for *All ELs*

A family enrolls their 7-year-old twins Amed and Qamaan into a U.S. public school for the first time. They indicate they speak Somali at home on the home language survey. The boys are administered a screener (a form of assessment) for their level of English proficiency and are eligible for language support. The parents are notified by a letter written in English that their children are eligible for language support services. This school does not offer an English/Somali bilingual program model, but they do offer a daily segment of English as a second language (ESL). The parents sign the required documents and assume their child will be offered language support in addition to general education. Unfortunately, the twins are never scheduled for language support and instead are placed into a general education second-grade class.

Ask yourself these questions:

- What happens now?
- What was supposed to happen, and why might the process have failed?
- Depending on your role, what would you do?

The aforementioned scenario describes a disconnect between when students are identified as ELs and the process by which they will begin to receive services. Although the students were identified within the expected time frame, it is not clear as to who needed to be notified, besides the parents, and how the person would be notified about new students eligible for language support. This scenario highlights not only the importance of who ELs are in your school but also the need for coherent procedures to ensure that services are provided.

Knowing Your ELs

Whether you are in a district with a high population of ELs or in a rural district with a relatively low number or ELs, understanding the complexities and rich diversity the population represents within a learning community is imperative. During a meeting with an elementary school principal, I quickly came to the realization that far more work was needed to support the school's EL population. The school, located in the northeastern part of the United States, was in a small town with a large EL population, mostly Spanish speakers. My contract with the district was for a limited number of days, and the district had already predetermined that this particular school was not its priority because of a number of other partnerships and programs being implemented. However, I believe that *all* schools with ELs are priorities. During the conversation, I asked the principal the number of students identified as EL in the school. He responded that he wasn't exactly sure. This was an unexpected response; school leaders must know specifics about their EL population and how to support those students. Though some school leaders know this information, there are others who do not. Without this information, discussions about school improvement efforts and student achievement are futile. The first step toward creating an equitable learning environment is knowing how ELs are defined and who the ELs are in your school.

English learner—The term "English learner," when used with respect to an individual, means an individual—(a) who is aged 3 through 21; (b) who is enrolled or preparing to enroll in an elementary school or secondary school; (c) (i) who was not born in the United States or whose native language is a language other than English; (ii) (I) who is a Native American or Alaska Native, or a native resident of the outlying areas; and (II) who comes from an environment where a language other than English has had a significant impact on the individual's level of English language proficiency; or (iii) who is migratory, whose native language is a language other than English, and who comes from an environment where a language other than English is dominant; and (d) whose difficulties in speaking, reading, writing, or understanding the English language may be sufficient to deny the individual—(i) the ability to meet the challenging State academic standards; (ii) the ability to successfully achieve in classrooms where the language of instruction is English; or (iii) the opportunity to participate fully in society (U.S. Department of Education, Non-Regulatory Guidance, 2016, p. 43).

State and local definitions of ELs may differ slightly. School leadership teams need to know how your state defines this population and the significance of such definitions. The more you engage in action-focused conversations that help build context around your particular population of ELs, the better and more sustainable your student achievement efforts will be. Essentially, there is no "one-size-fits-all" approach to this work: Your context matters!

Urgency in Action

The National Center for Educational Statistics reports 4.8 million ELs in U.S. public schools (U.S. Department of Education, National Center for Education Statistics, 2018). From a data perspective, national statistics about

Figure 1.1 Components of Leadership Practices for Linguistic Equity

Leadership Practices for Creating and Sustaining Linguistic Equity	
Meaningful Engagement and Shared Dialog with Teachers, Families and Staff	
Linguistic Civil Rights Language as a Right Federal Laws and Mandates	**Leading for Equity Knowledge Base** Culture as is relates to the community, district, school and students
Instructional Expertise Culturally Responsive Curriculum, Pedagogy and Assessment	**Staff Capacity Building** Hiring, Professional Development and Evaluation
Programs & Services Castañeda Three-Prong Approach, Implementation of Appropriate Program(s) Resources and Staffing, Effectiveness of Student Outcomes	**School Culture** Building trust, transparency, appreciation for linguistic diversity and community outreach

Source: Adapted from Callahan, DeMatthews, and Reyes (2019).

EL populations are alarming. They have been for a long time and remain so. Take, for example, the national graduation rates for ELs. In 2015–2016, the U.S. Department of Education reported graduation rates for ELs as 66.9%, nearly 20 percentage points lower than the 84.1% reported for all students. ELs were approximately 1% higher than only one subgroup—students with disabilities. The same year, only 2.8% of high school ELs participated in Scholastic Aptitude Test (SAT) or the American College Testing (ACT) exams, compared to 97.2% of non-ELs. These gaps exist across a number of content areas, yet we can get a false sense of security by believing that we are "doing what we can with what we have." I encourage you to examine the issues from a wide lens first, and then more granularly, as a way to be proactive and informed decision makers.

The need for school leaders to be more prepared for ELs has been the battle cry for decades. In her book on advocating for ELs, Staehr Fenner (2014) affirmed that "school administrators also find themselves unprepared to lead their teachers to teach ELs" (p. 13). Successfully supporting the academic achievement of ELs requires a "whole school" approach, because the needs of the students extend beyond just language as a potential barrier to understanding content. Misconceptions about linguistic diversity, racial identity, cultural diversity, citizenship, and how one might feel included (or excluded) within a learning community can pose persistent challenges that affect ELs' language instruction and overall sense of belonging. Though research on effective principal characteristics and the principal's role in increasing student achievement exists, there has been very little research on supporting principals' depth of knowledge around linguistic equity. Callahan, DeMatthews, and Reyes (2019) provide a framework for linguistic equity "as [the] core of effective leadership practices: (a) instructional expertise, (b) teacher/staff capacity building, (c) programs and services, and (d) school culture" (p. 282). Figure 1.1 provides an illustration of the components of linguistic equity.

Additionally, to create a catalyst for change, school leaders must first confront their own biases and knowledge gaps about minority student populations (Bryan, Cooper, & Ifarinu, 2019, p. 199; Singleton & Linton, 2006, p. 5). Such self-reflection is necessary before school leaders are able to create and sustain inclusive school communities for all students, particularly ELs. This reflection allows educators to acknowledge the beliefs, behaviors, and practices they have that may interfere with student interactions. Hammond (2015) refers to this as doing the "inside-out" work (p. 53). Dormer poses questions to school leaders that get at the heart of matter:

> What happens when uninformed teachers make statements or engage in actions that are perceived as threatening or discriminatory to immigrant families or international students? And what is the result of ELLs spending a majority of their school time in high stress conditions as a result of a pervasive lack of understanding of the realities of language acquisition? And what about the potential for linguistic, racial, and ethnic divisions in schools when a culture embracing diversity is not fostered? (Dormer, 2016, p. 2).

Dormer (2016) is asking about the conditions—in this case, high stress that we either create or that exists as part of school communities. In order to combat these conditions and create ones that are more conducive to learning, supporting ELs by creating a sense of urgency is imperative. For that sense of urgency to be sustained long term, it must be woven into the fabric of the school community. Soto's (2012) research on EL shadowing affirms how the achievement gap between traditionally marginalized groups of children (e.g., Latino, African American, and ELs) compared to native English speakers is a moral and ethical imperative (p. 4). Failing to address achievement gaps sets the stage for these violations. Forte and Faulkner-Bond (2010) affirm, "Where failure to meet the needs of these students amounts to a violation of such rights, school systems much adopt practices to correct that violation or prevent students from experiencing discrimination" (p. 2). Without an understanding of key approaches for supporting ELs, decisions could be made, albeit unintentionally, allowing practices that create flawed or problematic learning contexts for linguistically diverse learners.

State- and district-level responsibilities for linguistically diverse students date back to the 1920s (Forte & Faulkner-Bond, 2010, p. 2). Civil and constitutional rights are the foundation for the legislation that follows.

Table 1.1 Landmark Cases

***Mendez v. Westminster School District* (1946)**	Mexican-Americans filed a lawsuit against the Westminster School District in Orange County, California for segregation practices, such as having "Mexican Schools" for Mexican students.
***Brown v. Board of Education* (1954)**	Supreme Court case in which the justices unanimously ruled racial segregation of children in public schools was unconstitutional.
***Title VI of the Civil Rights Act* (1964)**	Districts must take affirmative steps to ensure that English learners can meaningfully participate in their educational programs and services.
***Lau v. Nichols* (1974)**	Supreme Court case in which Chinese-American students in San Francisco filed a lawsuit against the district for proficiency English as a graduation requirement although the district was not providing support for students to become proficient in English.
***Castañeda v. Pickard* (1981)**	Fifth Circuit Court ruling that established a three-part test to evaluate bilingual programs. Local education agencies must provide English learners with English language development programs that are based on sound educational theory, provided with staff and resources in a manner "reasonably calculated" for program success, and evaluated regularly and revised where needed.
Plyler v. Doe (1982)	Supreme Court case that ruled states are required to provide free public education to students regardless of citizenship status.

Table 1.1 illustrates a timeline of landmark cases involving equity and access to education for ELs. All of these cases build on the U.S. Constitution 14th Amendment Equal Protection Clause (1868), which says that "no state shall deny any person equal protection under the law, which includes discriminatory practices and the provision of equal opportunity."

Decades later, with the Every Student Succeeds Act (ESSA) in 2015, federal law for the first time held schools accountable for ELs' progress toward proficiency in English and academic achievement in content areas. Although ELs are highlighted as part of the mandate, the law does not come without challenges, in particular regarding interpretation and implementation. Some of the challenges with ESSA and EL accountability include knowing how your state determines the size for an EL subgroup, how the state determines proficiency in English, how and what goals will be used to determine success rates, and the maximum number of years allowed to reach proficiency. Because states have autonomy over how these areas are described and implemented, monitoring and cross-comparisons are difficult.

The 2015 "Dear Colleague Letter" issued by the U.S. Department of Justice and the U.S. Department of Education identified 10 common Civil Rights issues. These issues included failing to do or provide the following for ELs:

- Identification and assessment of language needs in a timely manner

- A service model that is educationally sound and research based

- Sufficient staff for language programs

- Equal opportunity for ELs to participate in school- and district-wide programs

- Avoiding unnecessary segregative practices and program models

- Identifying ELs with disabilities and including their language needs in evaluation and services offered

- Meeting the needs of ELs who waive language support programs

- Monitoring of ELs who have reached proficiency

- Monitoring and evaluation of language programs and student progress

- Communication with parents

(U.S. Department of Justice & U.S. Department of Education, 2015, p. 8)

In addition to identifying ELs and programmatic concerns, school leaders must also recognize the social, emotional, academic, and language needs of ELs, which are quite diverse. ELs are not a monolithic group. Their experiences in U.S. public schools are as diverse as their cultural backgrounds. For example, an EL in an urban school district with a large population of ELs may have more resources and more access to effective program models than a student in a rural school district with a small population of ELs. ELs' ages upon entering U.S. schools, their prior lack of experiences with school, the preparedness of their teachers, and the service models they are afforded are all contributing factors to their success in school.

Take, for example, a small subgroup of ELs who are also identified as students with interrupted formal education (SIFEs). This label most often applies to those who are newly arrived to the United States during adolescence and could be immigrants or refugees. Typically, SIFEs have needs that are not met in traditional ESL programs. Some of those challenges include no or limited literacy skills in their native language; being older, more mature than the students in the programs in which they are placed; and social emotional needs that have not addressed. Although not all SIFEs are ELs, those who are may "literally run out of time to complete the requirements for high school graduation before the state-determined time to attend public school" (Custodio & O'Loughlin, 2017, p. 12). The sense of limited time to meet the needs of secondary ELs has been noted in a research conducted by Short and Fitzsimmons (2007), who indicate that ELs in middle and high schools must do double the work, learning English and content simultaneously while ultimately being held as accountable as their native-English-speaking peers.

Assets-Based, Culturally Responsive Schools

For school leaders to understand and act upon the civil rights aspects of supporting ELs, they must be unbiased and committed to assuring linguistic equity and access for all learners in their schools. Part of developing this level of awareness is understanding one's own culture and the culture of an American school. Schools have a culture that may be different from the home culture of the linguistically diverse students they serve. Similarities or differences between the two cultures can be a huge place of impact, depending on how school leaders manage their schools. This largely depends upon approaches used to bring home and school cultures together. If a deficit-based approach is used, one that asserts the need to fix home cultures, then efforts will be wasted. Having a strength-based approach "requires a shift in our thinking from what we believe is lacking in our students to the many strengths and assets that they and their families already possess" (Zacarian & Staehr Fenner, 2020, p. 7). Students depend on their schools to provide them with academic learning experiences that they'll need for life. Hammond (2015) eloquently affirms that "dependent doesn't mean deficit" (p. 13). Just because ELs are dependent on their school communities to provide them with basic

Figure 1.2 Example District Approach to Supporting ELs

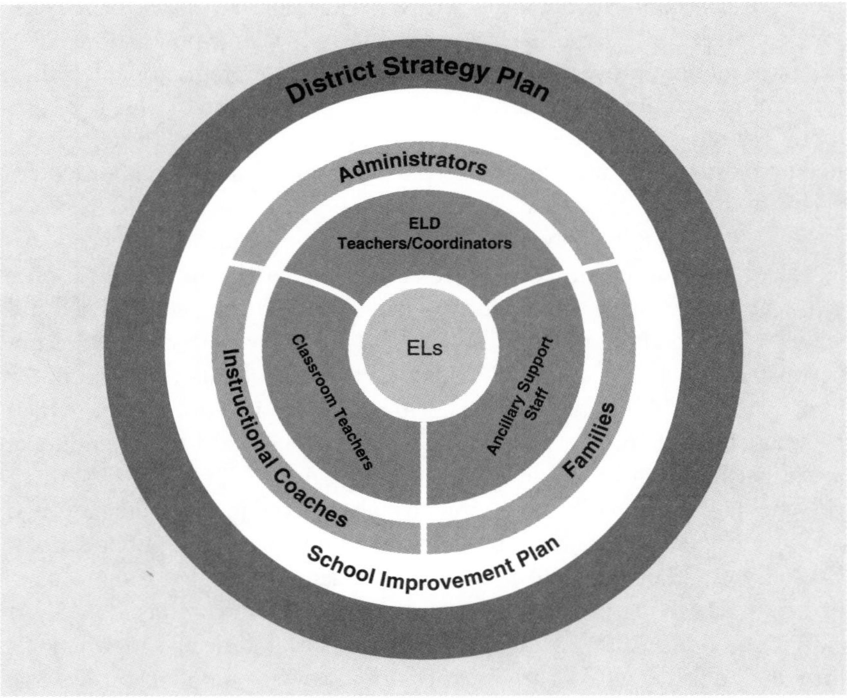

educational experiences, it doesn't mean they aren't engaging in other experiences that are of high importance and maturity, both moral and faith-based, within their communities and culture. Take, for example, a middle school that has small population of Muslim, Arabic-speaking ELs who are fasting during Ramadan. Would those students have to sit in the cafeteria during lunch time or could they meet in the media center instead? Regardless of the percentage of ELs, the size of the district, and the culture of the school community, ELs should be authentically included, recognized, and celebrated.

Figure 1.2 represents one district's approach to supporting ELs. Notice how the students, in the center, are supported by not only classroom teachers but also coordinators and ancillary staff members. Instructional coaches, administrators, and families are included around this core. Dove and Honigsfeld's (2018) research states the importance of educators not working in silos but rather collaboratively, with a focus on their EL population. This importance is underscored when you accept that "all teachers are teachers of ELs and responsible for supporting [ELs'] social-emotional well-being, acculturation, language development, and overall school success" (Dove & Honigsfeld, 2018, p. 3). It cannot be only the designated EL teachers who work to support ELs; EL student success—and therefore school and district success—hinges on all teachers working in unison.

Supporting ELs: Eight Important Questions

In order to begin action-oriented conversations about supporting ELs, school communities need to address the aforementioned considerations in a structured and systematic approach. This approach begins with the following questions:

Eight Questions that all School Leaders must be able to Answer about English Learners

1. How many students are identified as English learners in your school?
2. In which grade levels are your English learners?
3. What are their English language proficiency levels?
4. How many, if any, English learners are dually identified (i.e., English learners who are also gifted and/or have learning disabilities)?
5. How many teachers in the school are certified/endorsed to teach English learners?
6. What is the primary program model(s) of instruction in the school?
7. How many English learners have reached proficiency ("exited")?
8. How many of your English learners are being monitored once they have reached proficiency?

The remainder of this chapter examines each of these questions and the importance of answering them. These important questions serve, throughout this book, as the basis for further exploration of how school leaders can create and sustain effective learning communities for ELs.

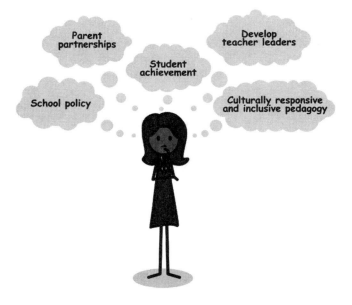

How Many Students Are Identified as ELs in Your School?

Determining the number of ELs in your school first requires an understanding of how students are identified as ELs. An example, provided in Figure 1.3, of an enrollment experience could look something like this: Families are asked to complete registration materials, such as a home language survey, which asks questions about the language(s) that are spoken in the home. If a family indicates that they speak another language besides English at home, their child may be eligible for language support services.

The flow chart in Figure 1.3 illustrates the steps involved in the identification process. What parents self-report on the home language survey is just the beginning; it is not what determines eligibility. If a language other than English is reported, then an English language screener must be administered. If English is the only language reported, there is no requirement to assess the student's English language proficiency. Depending on the state and/or district guidance, if a student has scored on the screener within the range needed to be eligible for language support services, he or she thereby acquires the label "English learner."

Once students are eligible for language support services, their parents or guardians could be presented with options for support. Though parents or guardians may waive or opt out of services for their child, there is no opting out of their children's participation in the annual English language proficiency exam.

Figure 1.3 Student Identification Flow Chart

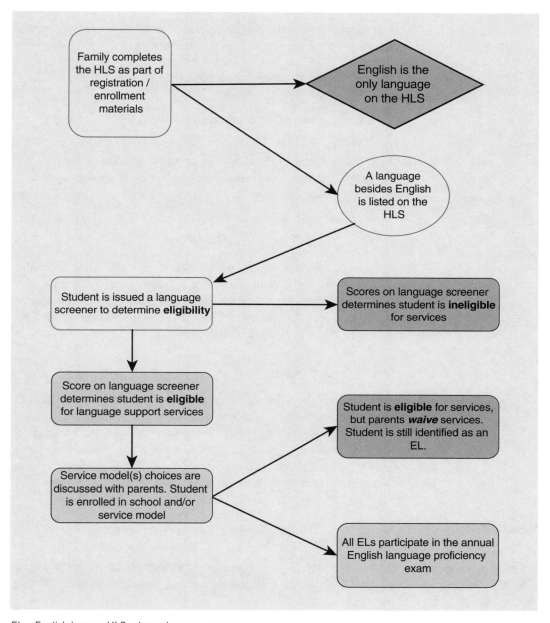

EL = English learner, HLS = home language survey.

Parents will be presented with options for program model choices, such as a bilingual or dual language model, or having a segment of time for English language development. This presentation of program choices is a critical time to educate parents and guardians about these options, because the misconceptions and misunderstandings about the services being offered can lead to confusion. (e.g., are dual language models the same as bilingual models?) For this reason, having interpreters available, especially during this process, is beneficial to all involved.

As a precursor to determining the number of ELs in a school, school leaders will want to answer the following questions:

- How many families indicated a language other than English as their primary home language?

- How many students were administered the English language proficiency screener?

- How many of the students who were administered the English language proficiency screener were eligible for language support services? How many were not eligible?

- How many of the students who were eligible for language support services waived or opted out of services?

The answers to these prequestions provide more context for determining your population of ELs. Until one is able to clearly identify their population of ELs, critical thinking about the needs of these students will remain vague. Once you know the number of ELs in your school, you are on your way to creating a truly inclusive learning community.

In Which Grade Levels Are Your ELs?

This question helps school leaders to have a clear picture of where the ELs are within the school community. Perhaps the ELs are evenly distributed across all grade levels, or perhaps they are clustered within a few grade levels. You may even have only one or two ELs in a particular grade level. Mapping where your ELs fall within grade levels allows you to begin appropriately supporting student achievement.

Table 1.2 Example Student Population: School A

Grade	Number of English Learners
K	34
1	28
2	22
3	17
4	11
5	5
Total	117

Table 1.3 Example Student Population: School B

Grade	Number of English Learners
K	16
1	9
2	3
3	0
4	1
5	0
Total	29

Tables 1.2 and 1.3 depict the EL population of two sample schools. Note that School A has a significantly larger population of ELs and a relatively even distribution of ELs across grade levels, whereas School B has a much smaller number of ELs (or zero) in select grade levels. These distributions could have implications with respect to planning for PL within the respective schools. Within a given year, School A leaders may take a school-wide approach to professional development (PD) with a focus on ELs. School B, however, may opt to support select grade levels, for example, kindergarten, in which the highest number of ELs are housed. Having a bird's-eye view of the students helps to form a macro to micro perspective of the population. This view also helps track trends in the population, such as decreases and increases over time.

What Are Their English Language Proficiency Levels?

School leaders and teachers need a clearer understanding of the process of becoming proficient in English. I've found that some educators believe that once students are identified as ELs, those students are consigned to this status throughout their schooling. This is not true. Although students may be learning English their entire lives, they can reach a level of English proficiency and be exited from the language support program. Our ultimate goal is to ensure that our students reach the highest level of English proficiency possible. Ideally, we'd like for students to become highly proficient in their native language and English, because the research is clear that maintaining and developing proficiency in a student's first language helps support learning a new language. There is no doubt that school leaders with a knowledge of second language acquisition, especially understanding how students develop proficiency, will be better equipped to support ELs. A good starting point for learning about language development is evaluating *your* level of proficiency in another language. You can do this by answering the following questions.

Proficiency Questionnaire		
1. Do you speak another language besides English as your **first** language?	Yes	No
If yes, what is your first language? _____		
2. Did you formally study a **second** language in high school and/or college?	Yes	No
		(Continued)

(Continued)

> If yes, what language did you study? _____

3. Think about your proficiency in your **second** language. In which domain of language (listening, speaking, reading, writing) are you **most proficient**?_____

4. Think about your proficiency in your **second** language. In which domain of language are you **least proficient**? _____

5. Do you consider yourself **proficient** in your **second** language?	Yes	No

 Available for download from **resources.corwin.com/justiceforels**

What these questions reveal about you as a language learner may or may not be new information for you. The questions encourage you to think about your own experience learning and gaining proficiency in a new language. They also encourage you to reflect on how you learned the new language. What was that experience like? Was it interactive, memorable, stressful, fun, challenging, and/or rewarding? Thinking back, was the experience what you wanted it to be? If not, what would you change about learning a new language? Perhaps it involved all of those emotions. For example, a school leader might answer the Proficiency Questionnaire the following way.

Proficiency Questionnaire: Sample Responses

1. Do you speak another language besides English as your **first** language? a. What is your first language? _English_	Yes	(No)
2. Did you formally study a **second** language, e.g., French or Spanish in high school and/or college? b. What language did you study? _French_	(Yes)	No

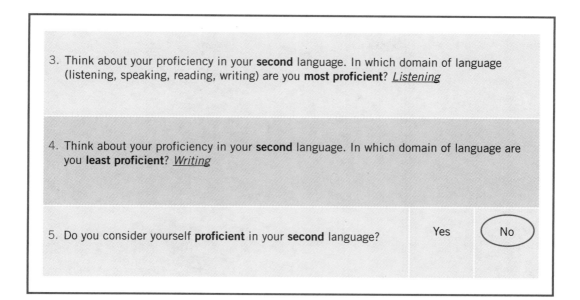

3. Think about your proficiency in your **second** language. In which domain of language (listening, speaking, reading, writing) are you **most proficient**? _Listening_

4. Think about your proficiency in your **second** language. In which domain of language are you **least proficient**? _Writing_

5. Do you consider yourself **proficient** in your **second** language?　　Yes　　(No)

Though the details of this leader's learning experience with French are missing, we know that this respondent self-identified as having a higher proficiency level in listening and a lower level in writing, and that she does not consider herself proficient in French. This example illustrates a key point about language development—that one can fall at different levels across the domains of language listening, speaking, reading, and writing. Similarly, a student's overall proficiency in English can be segmented by language domains.

An understanding of proficiency levels across grade levels will also increase your capacity to support your school's ELs. Recall that Table 1.2 showed the grade level distribution of the 117 ELs in Example School A. Figure 1.4 shows these students' English proficiency levels using a three-level scale of beginner, intermediate, and advanced.

Almost half of the students here are at the beginner level, slightly less than half are at the intermediate level, and the smallest number of students is at advanced level. With this information, school leaders can disaggregate each proficiency level by grade level. How many beginner, intermediate, and advanced level students are in each grade level? (See Table 1.4 for an example.)

In School A, there are 56 students at the beginner English language proficiency level. This information alone will assist school leaders in a number of areas, specifically with PD plans, curriculum, and instructional models. Presenting the data from a macro to micro perspective moves the conversation beyond instructional strategies: It also helps educators become intentional practitioners, those who are able to justify the "what" and "how" of the content being taught and expected from students at various levels of English language proficiency (Cooper, 2013).

Figure 1.4 Example Student English Proficiency Levels: School A

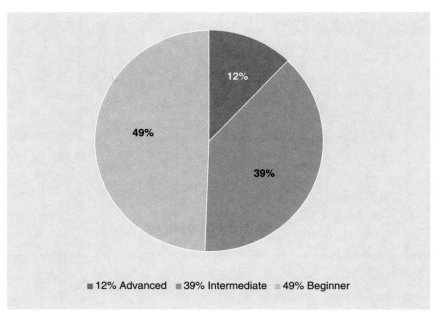

■ 12% Advanced   ■ 39% Intermediate   ■ 49% Beginner

Table 1.4 Example Student English Proficiency Levels by Grade: School A

Grade	Beginner	Intermediate	Advanced	Total
K	22	12	0	34
1	19	9	0	28
2	11	11	0	22
3	2	6	9	17
4	2	3	6	11
5	0	4	1	5
Total	**56**	**45**	**16**	**117**

The standards and assessments being used by your state work in tandem with how your state describes proficiency levels. For example, if your state is part of the WIDA Consortium (2012), then you would use the WIDA levels. Knowing what terms and phrases to use to describe proficiency can help educators understand second language acquisition and also allow them to plan curriculum and assessments with a focus on ELs. Table 1.5 shows some common English language descriptors used in the United States.

Table 1.5 Common English Language Descriptors Used in the United States

U.S.-Based Standards and Assessments	Member(s)	Language Descriptors
AZELLA	Arizona	Pre-Emergent (PE), Emergent (E), Basic (B) Low Intermediate (LI), High Intermediate (HI)
ELPAC	California	Levels 1–3; Novice, Intermediate, Initially Fluent
ELPA21	Arkansas, Iowa, Louisiana, Nebraska, Ohio, Oregon, Washington, West Virginia	Levels 1–5; Beginning, Early Intermediate, Intermediate,
LAS Links	Mississippi	Levels 1–5; Beginning, Early Intermediate, Intermediate, Proficient, Above Proficient
NYSESLAT	New York	Entering, Emerging, Transitioning, Expanding, Commanding
TELPAS	Texas	Beginning, Intermediate, Advanced, Advanced High
WIDA	Alabama, Alaska, Bureau of Indian Education, Colorado, Delaware, District of Columbia, Florida, Georgia, Hawaii, Idaho, Illinois, Indiana, Kentucky, Maine, Maryland, Massachusetts, Michigan, Minnesota, Missouri, Montana, Nevada, New Hampshire, New Jersey, New Mexico, North Carolina, North Dakota, Northern Mariana Islands, Oklahoma, Pennsylvania, Rhode Island, South Carolina, South Dakota, Tennessee, U.S. Virgin Islands, Utah, Vermont, Virginia, Wisconsin, Wyoming	Levels 1–6; Entering, Emerging, Developing, Expanding, Bridging, Reaching

Further information and discussion around language proficiency descriptors can be found in Chapter 2. Where are you located, and what is the assessment used to determine ELs' progress and attainment of proficiency? What proficiency descriptors are used in your state?

How Many, if Any, ELs Are Dually Identified?

Dually identified ELs—those who have learning disabilities and/or are gifted—are in the unique position of either being over- or underidentified. Some educators are surprised to find out which ELs are dually identified.

> I completed 5 of the 7 steps in order to investigate our population of ELs, identifying the number of ELs, grade, levels of [English language proficiency], dually identified, and students who are exited and monitored. I sent out the spreadsheet to my administrators and BAM! I got a huge response from everybody; they were surprised and kind of shocked with the breakdown. Especially out of 60 ELs, 26 are dually identified. **(High School Teacher, New Mexico)**

Aside from knowing the number of dually identified ELs, it is important to know the primary categories of disability. For example, if a school has a certain number of ELs with disabilities, how many have auditory processing disorder? Dyscalculia? Nonverbal learning disabilities? Sometimes, dually identified ELs are misdiagnosed as having a language processing disorder. Significantly, some educators have difficulty identifying the difference between a language disorder and the natural stages of second language acquisition. For example, is the EL displaying signs of selective mutism (an anxiety disorder), or is she in a "silent period"—a normal phase of language development?

Hamayan, Marler, Sánchez-López, and Damico (2013) state three areas that lead to the misidentification of special needs among ELs: (1) assessment practices, (2) an influence of the medical model when addressing educational issues, and (3) funding bias toward special education (p. 2). Once educators learn more about their dually identified population of ELs, they can collaborate more closely with their special education department.

It is the job of the special education team to coordinate special education student services with stakeholders. In one instance, a special education team leader confessed to me that she had not seen nor did she know how to analyze English language proficiency data. Understanding English language proficiency score reports was essential to her role in coordinating meetings to determine student eligibility for special education services. The same is true for determining eligibility for gifted programs. Programmatic pieces for dually identified ELs can no longer function separately from each other. Conversations about program models, appropriate services, and outcomes should be revisited once more educators are included, informed, and aware of students.

How Many Teachers in the School Are Certified/Endorsed to Teach ELs?

Whether they use bilingual, dual language, or ESL program models, schools suffer from a nationwide shortage of teachers who are prepared and qualified to teach ELs (Mitchell, 2018). This shortage also directly impacts general education settings. By completing a certification audit in their school, school leaders can have a quantitative measure of what licenses and endorsements their teachers hold. This information can also support PD initiatives or justify changes in initial PD plans. The following example from an executive director of elementary education in Georgia illustrates the problem with shortages in qualified EL teachers and increases in the EL student population:

> In 2016, in order to ease overcrowding in nearby schools, the school district initiated a process of redistricting the school attendance zones of multiple schools. As a result of this redistricting, our high school's enrollment increased from approximately 1300 students during the 2015-16 school year to approximately 1650 students during the 2016-17 school year. Of these approximately 350 additional students that enrolled in our school, most came from homes where English was not the predominant language spoken. Most of our new students' families from this redistricting process had recently immigrated to the United States from Guatemala, Mexico, El Salvador, and other Central American countries.

> As principal, in anticipation of this significant demographic shift in learner profile that our school was about to embark on, I knew that we needed to engage in proactive steps to build the capacity of our staff to serve the educational needs of students who were not proficient in English. At the time, out of 110 teachers on our school's faculty, only two had an ESOL endorsement associated with their teaching certification. [We had] our lone full time ESOL teacher and one of our Physical Education teachers. Additionally, over the course of the prior school year, my own formal and informal classroom observations of all 110 of our teachers demonstrated to me that our faculty had minimal understanding and limited efficacy with classroom instruction to support the genuine learning needs of students with limited English proficiency. (**Norman C. Sauce III, Ed.D. Executive Director of Elementary Education, former high school and elementary principal, Georgia. If Personal Communication, October 9, 2018**)

This school leader proactively responded to an increase of linguistically diverse learners. With only two staff members prepared to teach ELs, a school-wide PD plan with a focus on ELs was essential to the students' academic success. Simply ignoring this increase of ELs would have sent the message to staff to maintain the status quo—teaching to the middle. Instead, a clear message was sent to acknowledge the change in student population. In response to this change in population, the school helped prepare teachers to better understand and become more effective with their new students.

A certification audit may also encourage partnerships with other schools, districts, or institutes of higher education to support their own PD initiatives. For example, a principal of a high school in the southeast United States with a high number of ELs offered the ESOL endorsement to her staff on-site. The endorsement was offered by the Metropolitan Regional Educational Service Agency that served districts in the school's region. For a number of years, she encouraged staff members to earn their ESOL endorsements. Ultimately, she increased the number of staff members who were prepared to teach ELs by assisting them in obtaining ESOL endorsements and by sponsoring a cohort model that met at the school. The decisions made by these school leaders are two examples of concerted efforts by leaders to meet the needs of the students. These outcomes also helped to support learning communities in becoming more cognizant of the learners they serve.

Now that we know the importance of having qualified teachers of ELs, here are the steps for conducting a certification/licensure audit:

1. Survey the staff: Ask which licensures/endorsements they hold or are in the process of earning.

2. Ask which additional licenses/endorsements they would be interested in earning, if any.

3. Work with Human Resources to check licenses/endorsements of staff members.

4. Cross-analyze the results from the staff survey with the Human Resources audit.

5. Look for gaps in knowledge as they relate to teacher preparedness to teach ELs.

By conducting a certification audit, school leaders are assuring that they are not making decisions based on assumptions about PD needs; decisions will be made based on the needs of the staff and students, specifically ELs. The ultimate goal is to have as much specific information as possible in order to make the best PD plans that support student achievement.

What Is the Primary Program Model(s) of Instruction in the School?

Program models

A number of recommended language support program models exist. Often, program models are inherited from previous school administration; it would be optimistic to assume that school leaders are able to fully implement language programs from the ground up. Regardless of how a program model came to be, it's extremely important for a school leader to fully understand the model(s) that has been implemented in his or her school. Padron and Waxman's (2016) study asserted that "if bilingual/second language programs are to be effective in assisting children achieve academic success, then the school leadership must encourage and support the goals of the program" (p. 129). Bilingual and/dual language program models have had long-term proven results of academic student success. Although ideal, in certain contexts, these models may not be sustainable for a number of reasons. That does not mean that linguistic equity cannot be achieved nor does it mean that new and innovative models won't be effective. The more important question is whether program models are producing their intended results. (See Chapter 2 for more details about program models.)

Think about it: Can you fully articulate the language support program model in your school? I asked this question to a small group of ESOL teachers recently, and everyone was reluctant to answer. A few responded with hesitant answers in the form of a question, like, "We're pulling students out, right?" One teacher chimed in by confirming hers was a "block schedule" of time where students receive language support. When I asked what language instruction looked like during the block schedule, again, participants were reluctant to answer. Finally, one teacher described her class as a review of material being taught in other classes, including help with homework.

This question, "Can you fully articulate the language support program model in your school?", can be used to examine the instructional approaches used by school communities to primarily support English language development. Some common models include those in Table 1.6. (For a more extensive discussion of outcomes for these programs, see Chapter 2.)

School leaders must know and be able to articulate their English language program model as well as describe the vision and mission of the program.

Table 1.6 Common Program Models in the United States

Program Model	Description
ESL (English as a second language)	ESL class may be scheduled as a block class or multiple classes (e.g., ESL I, ESL II).
Cotaught	ESL and general education teachers coteach within a general education setting.
Small Group Push-In	ESL teachers serve students in their general education classes by working with selected ELs individually or in small groups for a specific period of time (e.g., daily or on specified days).
Small Group Pull-Out	ESL teachers serve a small group of students outside of their general education classes for a specific period of time (e.g., daily or on specified days).
Bilingual Education	Two languages are used to develop proficiency in the target language. This model typically uses each language for a certain percentage of the day. (e.g., an 80/20 model would use English for 80% and the second language for 20% of the day.)
Dual Language	Two languages are being taught to develop proficiency in both languages. This model can include native English speakers and ELs.
Sheltered Instruction	Content courses are taught by teachers who have been trained to differentiate instruction so that ELs have access to content concepts.

Curriculum

Curriculum is the other piece of EL program model that is important for school leaders to understand. Think about the curriculum being used in your school. Is this curriculum being used to teach ELs and, if so, to what extent is it being differentiated through a language learning lens? For example, a district purchases a new curriculum. There are some areas that address ELs, but these usually appear in the margins of the curriculum guide and are presented as "quick tips" or "strategies." The curriculum does not go deep enough to address content and language development. This leaves teachers frustrated and requesting more strategies, more differentiated teaching materials, and more time to plan and create informal assessments for teaching ELs. Do any of these requests sound familiar?

Program assessment

Ubben, Hughes, and Norris (2016) state, "The ELL programs need to provide a challenging curriculum, use appropriate language development components, and incorporate good assessment approaches" (p. 175). The need for both formal and informal English language program evaluations allows school leaders to understand the day-to-day inner workings of their school's language program vs. a one-time audit event for compliance.

Here are some questions to help you informally evaluate your EL program model:

- What are your strengths as a department/program?

- What are some of your recent successes?

- What do you want ELs to be able to know and do as a result of participating in this program?

- How do your efforts align with the district's goals, mission, and vision?

- How are your efforts as a department communicated to stakeholders?

This situation presents a number of variables with no quick solutions. One must first recognize the mother's sense of urgency around understanding her child's progress. Retention of an EL is already problematic because we don't know if it is primarily the content, the student's level of English, the instruction received, or all of those factors that led to the child being retained in the first place. The principal's decision will have implications, regardless of the choice. The question is: Which choice is best for the student in both the short and long term? Will the parents feel validated by the principal's decision, or will they feel marginalized? In order for the principal to make the best decision for the student, he or she would have to take into account

January 20XX

A first grade student's parents, Mr. and Mrs. Suarez, want their child removed from the bilingual class and placed into a general education class. The child has been retained and is repeating first grade. The mother speaks Spanish and the father speaks both English and Spanish. The mother's primary concern is that her son is not progressing in his reading ability in English. His proficiency in English is at an intermediate level. Should he stay in his class or should he be moved to a general education class?

_____

_____

_____

_____

the parent's wishes, include the teachers, and have some evidence that supports the final decision.

How Many ELs Have Reached Proficiency?

Understanding how ELs in your district and school are considered proficient in English is equally as important as knowing who your ELs are. In PL sessions that I facilitate, this question comes up almost every time: "How do you define proficiency in English in your state?" Educators that I encounter are not usually able to answer that question. Looks of confusion, doubt, and silence usually follow.

The ideal English learning path would lead to an EL becoming proficient in English while maintaining his or her native language. However, this goal (proficiency) requires definition. If the majority of educators don't know or understand what the goal is, or the process to get there, then how can they be prepared to help students reach proficiency? Thus, a clear understanding of your state's exit criteria is essential knowledge for ensuring that ELs are properly identified, supported, *and* exited from your program.

Based on their English language assessments scores, for students who have not reached proficiency but who were close, additional guiding questions should be raised:

- How close were they to reaching proficiency?

- Was the format of the testing an issue? For example, if the language assessment is administered online, did the student demonstrate any frustrations with navigating the online platform?

- What is the program model that was applied? Did the student opt out of services?

- Who are the student's teachers, and have they analyzed this student's English language proficiency?

- What types, if any, of differentiated instruction have been utilized?

You can see here that progress toward proficiency is just as important as reaching proficiency. By that, I mean we can celebrate those who have reached proficiency just as we can those who are making progress. For both groups, what next steps will be in place to continue supporting the student appropriately? In order to answer these questions and move forward, conversations around supporting all students, but especially those who are at high levels of English proficiency, are necessary.

Once ELs have reached proficiency, they are exited from their language program and moved to a status often referred to as "monitored"; they may still need additional support with certain content areas, just as native-English-speaking students might.

How Many of Your ELs Are Being Monitored Once They Have Reached Proficiency?

In their 2015 "Dear Colleague Letter," the U.S. Department of Justice and the U.S. Department of Education state that state education agencies and school districts must "monitor exited students to ensure they were not prematurely exited and that any academic deficits incurred in the language assistance program have been remedied" (p. 8). What monitoring looks like depends upon what systems and structures your district has in place. When students are moved to monitored status, they are sometimes referred to as M1 or M2 (for Monitored Year 1 or Monitored Year 2). In some districts, students are monitored through their report cards, collaborative meetings, data management systems, or a combination of those. Monitoring does not have to be an elaborate process, but there must be a process in place. Though the U.S. Department of Education mandates that monitoring must occur, it does not mandate any particular monitoring model or program to monitor students.

The worst-case scenario (which, unfortunately, is not uncommon) is one in which school leaders and teachers are not aware of a former EL's monitored status at all. In such cases, efforts to continue supporting former ELs are not part of conversations around student achievement. A major myth that exists is that once ELs reach proficiency, they no longer need support. This is not true. Consider your general education native-English-speaking student. Many of these students need various supports at different points of their educational career. The same is true for students learning English; for example, former ELs may struggle with abstract concepts as part of an algebra or a chemistry course. Depending on their learning experiences, learning style, motivation to learn, and the like, they, too, may need support to continue having access to content. The issue here may not be their level of English proficiency but rather their understanding of advanced content concepts.

Figure 1.5 School Level English Language Development Plan

Building Level English Language Development Plan

School_____ SY_____

Principal_____

How will you service the students at level 1 and 2 English level proficiency in your building to ensure they receive intensive instruction in English language development over and above content?

How will you service the students at level 3 and 4 English level proficiency in your building to ensure they receive instruction over and above the content in order to give them the opportunity to gain the skills needed to score proficient? (5)

How will you progress monitor the development of your students' English Language proficiency?

Explain how you plan to include the ELD teacher and data in your content level PLC conversations.

Who will be at the IEP meeting when an EL also has a disability in order to address the language proficiency support/needs and what information will be shared with the team?

List two specific Professional Development needs for your administration, clerical staff, or instructional staff the MCS department can provide to ensure an equitable educational learning environment for your students and families.

Source: Karen Gracia Brown

Table 1.7 Common Civil Rights Issues Aligned to the Eight Questions for School Leaders of English Learners

Common Civil Rights Issues	Eight Questions for School Leaders
Identification and assessment of language needs in a timely manner	1. How many students are identified as ELs in your school? 2. In which grade levels are your ELs? 3. What are their English language proficiency levels?
A service model that is educationally sound and research based	6. What are the primary program model(s) of instruction in the school?
Sufficient staff for language programs	5. How many teachers in the school are certified/endorsed to teach ELs?
Equal opportunity for ELs to participate in school- and district-wide programs	2. In which grade levels are your ELs? 6. What are the primary program model(s) of instruction in the school?
Avoiding unnecessary segregative practices and program models	2. In which grade levels are your ELs? 6. What are the primary program model(s) of instruction in the school?
ELs with disabilities are identified and their language needs are included in evaluation and services offered	4. How many, if any, ELs are dually identified?
Meeting the needs of ELs who waive language support programs	1. How many students are identified as ELs in your school? 2. In which grade levels are your ELs?
Monitoring of ELs who have reached proficiency	7. How many ELs have reached proficiency ("exited")? 8. How many of your ELs are being monitored once they have reached proficiency?
Monitor and evaluation of language programs and student progress	6. What are the primary program model(s) of instruction in the school?
Communication with parents	Questions 1–8

*EL = English learner

Bringing It All Together

Some districts have begun the work of moving beyond compliance by supporting principals at the school level. This requires a closer look at what happens within each school and allowing for creative approaches to challenges. Table 1.7 shows how the questions on page 11 are directly aligned to the common civil rights issues. After being asked those questions, one district leader created a document called the School *Level English Language Development Plan* to guide conversations with school principals who have ELs in their schools (Figure 1.5). This document allows for more explicit

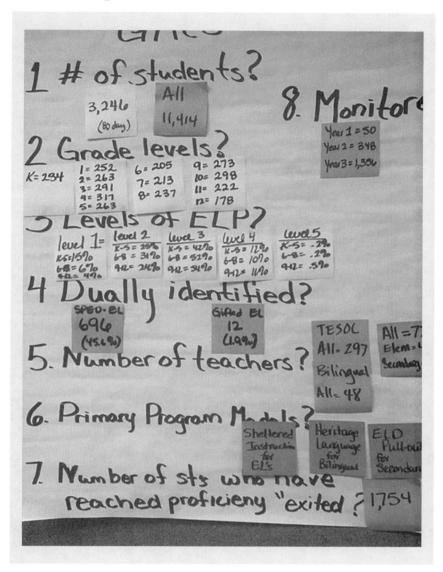

explanations of how ELs are being supported, as opposed to the more typical checkbox approach for compliance. This document also supports principals in thinking about developing a sharper understanding of EL programs within their schools. Figure 1.6 depicts how one school leader organized her answers to the eight questions on chart paper as part of a PL exercise for school leaders. In the next chapter of the book, we look closer at the issues related to program models for ELs and how we can support school leaders in understanding and advocating for what is in place at their schools.

FOLLOW-UP QUESTIONS ....

1. Which of the eight questions on page 11 were you able to answer *before* reading the chapter?

2. Which questions could you answer *after* reading the chapter?

3. Which questions did you find most challenging to answer? Why?

4. How will answering these questions begin to help you as a school leader?

5. How will answering these questions begin to help instructional coaches, teachers, and support personnel in your school?

6. Who else needs to be part of the question/answer process?

7. What are the next steps you will take to create more awareness in your school?

8. What new questions have come about as a result of this inquiry?

9. How will you go about prioritizing the areas in need of attention?

10. What additional supports, if any, will you need in order to complete your action plan?

FURTHER GUIDANCE AND SUPPORT RESOURCES ....

Websites

- Colorín Colorado (www.colorincolorado.org)

- English Learner Success Forum (www.elsuccessforum.org)

- National Association of English Learner Program Administrators (www.naelpa.org)

- National Clearinghouse for English Language Acquisition (ncela.ed.gov)

- U.S. Department of Education Office of English Language Acquisition (ncela.ed.gov)

Blogs

- Colorín Colorado (www.colorincolorado.org/blog)

- Corwin Connect (corwin-connect.com/category/english-language-learners)

- ELLEvation EL Community (ellevationeducation.com/ell-community/type/blog)

- EXC-ELL (exc-ell.com/blog)

- SupportEd (getsupported.net/blog)

- Zacarian Associates (zacarianconsulting.com/newsletter)

- TESOL International Association (blog.tesol.org)

Additional Readings

- *Language Magazine* (www.languagemagazine.com)

- Regional Education Laboratory Program (ies.ed.gov/ncee/edlabs/projects /english_learners.asp)

- Understanding Language (ell.stanford.edu/papers/practice)

REFERENCES ·····

Brown v. Board of Education, 347 U.S. 483 (1954).

Bryan, K., Cooper, A., Ifarinu, B. (2019). From Majority to Minority Advocating for English Learners from the African Diaspora. In H. Linville & J. Whiting (Eds.), *Advocacy in English language teaching and learning* (pp.190–201). New York, NY: Routledge.

Callahan, R., DeMatthews, D., & Reyes, P. (2019). The impact of Brown on EL students: Addressing linguistic and educational rights through school leadership practice and preparation. *Journal of Research on Leadership Education, 14*(4), 281–307. doi:10.1177/1942775119878464

Castañeda v. Pickard, 648 F.2d 989 (1981).

Civil Rights Act, Title VI Statute, 42 U.S.C (1964).

Cooper, A. (2013, August 1). *Using writing prompts with ELLs: My summer vacation (Part 3) [Blog post]*. Retrieved from http://colorincolorado.org/blog/using -writing-prompts-ells-my-summer-vacation-part-3

Custodio, B. K., & O'Loughlin, J. B. (2017). *Students with interrupted formal education: Bridging where they are and what they need*. Thousand Oaks, CA: SAGE.

Dormer, J. E. (2016). *What school leaders need to know about English learners*. Alexandria, VA: TESOL Press.

Dove, M. G., & Honigsfeld, A. (2018). *Co-teaching for English learners: a guide to collaborative planning, instruction, assessment, and reflection*. Thousand Oaks, CA: Corwin Press.

Forte, E., & Faulkner-Bond, M. (2010). *The administrator's guide to federal programs for English learners*. Washington, DC: Thompson.

Hamayan, E. V., Marler, B., Sánchez-López, C. S., & Damico, J. (2013). *Special education considerations for English language learners: Delivering a continuum of services*. Philadelphia, PA: Caslon.

Hammond, Z. (2015). *Culturally responsive teaching and the brain: Promoting authentic engagement and rigor among culturally and linguistically diverse students*. Thousand Oaks, CA: Corwin Press.

Lau v. Nichols, 414 U.S. 563 (1974).

Mendez v. Westminster School Dist., 64 F. Supp. 544 (S.D. Cal. 1946).

Mitchell, C. (2018, January 25). *The National Shortage of ELL Teachers Has Caught the Eye of Congress*. Retrieved from http://blogs.edweek.org/edweek/learning -the-language/2018/01/solve_ell_teacher_shortage.html

Padron, Y., & Waxman, H. (2016). Investigating principals' knowledge and perceptions of second language programs for English language learners. *International Journal of Educational Leadership and Management, 4*(2), 127–146.

Plyler v. Doe, 457 U.S. 202 (1982).

Short, D., & Fitzsimmons, S. (2007). *Double the work: Challenges and solutions to acquiring language and academic literacy for adolescent English language learners*. Washington, DC: Alliance for Excellent Education.

Singleton, G. E., & Linton, C. (2006). *Courageous conversations about race: A field guide for achieving equity in schools*. Thousand Oaks, CA: Corwin Press.

Soto, I. (2012). *ELL shadowing as a catalyst for change*. Thousand Oaks, CA: Corwin Press.

Staehr Fenner, D. (2014). *Advocating for English learners: A guide for educators*. Thousand Oaks, CA: Corwin Press.

Ubben, G. C., Hughes, L. W., & Norris, C. J. (2016). *The principal: Creative leadership for excellence in schools* (8th ed.). Upper Saddle River, NJ: Pearson Education.

U.S. Constitution 14th Amendment Equal Protection Clause, § 3. (1868).

U.S. Department of Education & Non-Regulatory Guidance. (2016). *English learners and Title III of the Elementary and Secondary Education Act (ESEA), as amended by the Every Student Succeeds Act (ESSA), Non-Regulatory Guidance: English Learners and Title III of the Elementary and Secondary Education Act (ESEA), as amended by the Every Student Succeeds Act (ESSA)1–48*. Washington, DC: Author.

U.S. Department of Education, National Center for Education Statistics. (2018, April). *English language learners in public schools*. Retrieved from https://nces .ed.gov/programs/coe/indicator_cgf.asp

U.S. Department of Justice & U.S. Department of Education. (2015). *Dear colleague letter: English learner students and limited English proficient parents*. Retrieved from https://www2.ed.gov/about/offices/list/ocr/letters/colleague -el-201501.pdf

WIDA Consortium. (2012). *2012 Amplification of the English language development standards: Kindergarten–grade 12*. Madison, WI: Board of Regents of the University of Wisconsin System.

Zacarian, D., & Staehr Fenner, D. (2020). From deficit-based to assets-based. In M. E. Calderon, M. G. Dove, D. S. Fenner, M. Gottlieb, A. M. Honigsfeld, T. W. Singer, . . .D. Zacarian, *Breaking down the wall: Essential shifts for English learners' success* (pp. 1–20). Thousand Oaks, CA: Corwin Press.

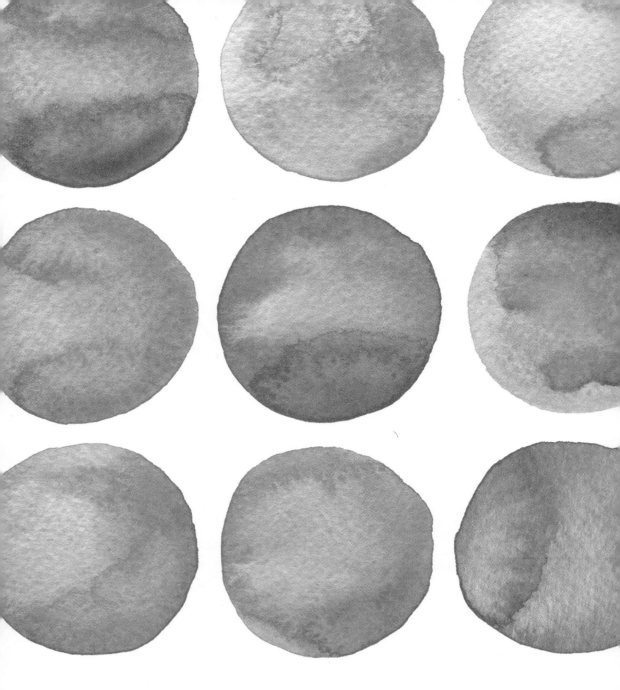

*English language program models
with similar names may be completely different.
That can be confusing!*

Program Models for English Learners: What's Happening in Your School?

Scenario: Selecting Appropriate Service Models for English Learners

A first-grade student, Fatima, enrolls in a new school year midyear. Her home language is Arabic. The language screener indicates Fatima is at a beginner level of English proficiency. The English language support model offered at her school is bilingual education in Grades K–3 and a sheltered instruction model in Grades 4 and 5. A daily segment of English language development (ELD) is offered across all grade levels. The dilemma is that the bilingual classes are English and Spanish. There are two options for Fatima. She can be placed into the bilingual English/Spanish first-grade class or a general education first-grade class with a segment of ELD support. As the school leader, which model would you suggest to her parents or guardian? How would you explain the program options to her parents or guardians? What are the expected academic outcomes for Fatima as she completes the reminder of the year at your school?

The preceding scenario is an example of how situations arise daily where decisions must be made in the best interest of the student, but the implications of those decisions can have long-term effects, both positive and negative. Which program model do you think is best for Fatima? In her particular case, the bilingual teacher who completed Fatima's intake forms and administered the English screener placed her into the bilingual English/Spanish class. Why she chose that class, we don't know. Perhaps she thought she could offer Fatima more support in that particular class? Maybe she thought Fatima would not do as well in a general education class with a segment of ELD support? Although the school leader was not directly involved in the registration and class placement process, the school leader is still responsible for the student's academic success; this is why a school leader's full understanding of his or her school's language support program models matter!

This chapter provides descriptions of some of the most common English language program models in K–12 settings along with considerations to assure the best possible outcomes for students.

Adhering to Federal Guidance

Part of the federal guidance around program models for English learners (ELs) as outlined in the "Dear Colleague Letter" (U.S. Department of Justice & U.S. Department of Education, 2015) states the following:

> Language assistance services or programs for EL students must be educationally sound in theory and effective in practice; however, the civil rights laws do not require any particular program or method of instruction for EL students. Students in EL programs must receive appropriate language assistance services until they are proficient in English and can participate meaningfully in the district's educational programs without language assistance services. (p. 12)

The wording can become challenging for educators to interpret, particularly the phrase "any particular program or method." It would be a falsehood to say that all school leaders have the opportunity to design and implement the best English language program models for their students. In many cases, program models may have been implemented for years, and leaders may not be familiar, or even acquainted with, what particular models are in place at their schools. There are those that have always been "done this way," and also those that may be more fluid and innovative. In any case, ideal program models evolve over time in direct response to student needs, meet federal guidelines, and are educationally sound and effective. The federal guidance also cautions educators to "avoid unnecessary segregation of EL students" (U.S. Department of Justice & U.S. Department of Education, 2015, p. 8). Although specialized language courses that are conducted separately from the general education course offerings may be necessary for a particular period of time, these courses must be designed to support overall student success. Schools cannot "retain EL students in EL-only classes for periods longer or shorter than required by each student's level of English proficiency, time and progress in the EL program, and the stated goals of the EL program" (U.S. Department of Justice & U.S. Department of Education, 2015, p. 23). An example of such unnecessary segregation would be if ELs were in English as a second language (ESL) leveled courses for a large part of or their entire educational career. Another example would be if course schedules were designed in a way that kept ELs out of advanced courses and/or extracurricular activities.

Design and intent of English language support programs matter! As affirmed by Sugarman (2018), "critically analyzing the design and implementation of a school's EL instructional model is an important step in school-improvement efforts that aim to boost EL outcomes and ensure an equitable education for all" (p. 14). In order for school leaders to be able to support and monitor the programs in their schools to ensure the programs are indeed adhering to their goals—and to federal guidelines—the leaders need to fully understand what these programs are and how they are being implemented.

Program Models

A number of approved English language program models exist. Some are highly self-functioning while others are in need of support, depending upon their context and implementation. Some schools may be fortunate enough to have more than one model in place. Table 2.1 provides a brief description of some common program models and expected outcomes from those programs. The more responsive the program model(s) are to student needs, the better the expected outcomes are.

Table 2.1 Descriptions and Outcomes of Common Program Models in the United States

Program Model and Grade Levels Most Associated With Them	Program Description	Expected Outcomes
ESL (K–12)	ESL class may be scheduled as a block class or multiple classes (e.g., ESL I, ESL II). This model is also referred to as "English immersion"	Students are taught in the target language with support provided in their native language as needed. Students are working toward attaining English proficiency.
Cotaught (K–8)	ESL and general education teachers coteach within a general education setting. This model is a form of "English immersion."	Instruction is provided in the target language by two teachers using a variety of coteaching techniques. Support in the students' native language may be provided as students work toward attaining English proficiency.
Small Group Push-In (K–8)	ESL teachers serve students in their general education classes by working with selected ELs individually or in small groups for a specific period of time (e.g., daily or on specified days). This model is a form of "English immersion."	Instruction is provided in the general education classroom by the ESL teacher for a period of time in the target language. Small groups may be composed of ELs with similar levels of proficiency or with mixed levels of proficiency. Support in the students' native language may be provided as students work toward attaining English proficiency.
Small Group Pull-Out (K–8)	ESL teachers serve a small group of students outside of their general education classes for a specific period of time (e.g., daily or on specified days). This model is a form of "English immersion."	Instruction is provided outside of the general education classroom by the ESL teacher for a period of time in the target language. Small groups may be composed of ELs with similar levels of proficiency or with mixed levels of proficiency. Support in the students' native language may be provided as students work toward attaining English proficiency.

(Continued)

Table 2.1 (Continued)

Program Model and Grade Levels Most Associated With Them	Program Description	Expected Outcomes
Bilingual Education (K–8)	Two languages are used to develop proficiency in the target language. This model typically uses each language for a certain percentage of the day. (e.g., an 80/20 model would use English for 80% and the second language for 20% of the day.) This model is also a form of "One-way, two-way, or transitional bilingual education."	Instruction and supports are provided for ELs in two languages with the goal of assisting students in maintaining their native language while students work toward attaining English proficiency. Students typically spend their day in the same class with the same students and are taught by the same teachers.
Dual Language (K–8)	Two languages are being taught to develop proficiency in both languages. This model can include both native English speakers and ELs.	Instruction and supports are provided in two languages with the goal of assisting students in developing proficiency in two languages. Students in this model can be a combination of ELs and native English speakers. Students typically spend their day in the same class with the same students and are taught by the same teachers.
Sheltered Instruction (K–12)	Content courses are taught by teachers who have been trained to differentiate instruction so that ELs have access to content concepts while developing academic language proficiency in English. This model is a form of "English immersion."	Students are taught in the target language with support provided in their native language as needed. Students are working toward attaining English proficiency.

EL = English learner; ESL = English as a second language.

Some state and local education agency-approved English program models may be offered that are considered an alternative to existing programs. For example, alternative models for language support may be in the form of an extended school day, after school tutoring, and summer enrichment. Such models allow for more creativity and flexibility and are just as responsive to student needs as the aforementioned program models when implemented with fidelity *and* as intended.

Program Model Considerations

Regardless of which program model(s) are in place at your school, it is imperative that unnecessary segregatory practices are avoided. Even with the best intentions, program models that are not well designed, not responsive to student needs, and not fully supported put students at risk for failure through no fault of their own. Educators who design, implement, and evaluate English language programs must keep the needs of the students they serve on the forefront of those initiatives.

Newcomer Programs

Newcomer programs or centers are geared toward supporting ELs who are new arrivals to U.S. public schools. These are more common for ELs in secondary school settings. Newcomer programs or centers encompass a range of possibilities. Classes could be as short as a brief block that students attend daily or as long as a full-day model where students spend a certain amount of time (e.g., 1 month up to 1 year) before being transitioned into another English language service model. This model can be implemented within a traditional school or housed at a separate location where students are transported to receive services.

What makes newcomer programs or centers distinctly different from other language programs is that they are usually for a select period of time and for older ELs at lower levels of English proficiency upon enrollment. Martin and Suárez-Orozco's (2018) research on newcomer programs in the United States and Sweden found common practices among highly effective newcomer programs. The schools studied were described as

> rich with innovations and workarounds within the confines of restrictive district, state, and national policies of standardization and unequal funding formulas. Their approaches were both comprehensive as well as individualized, led by passionate and insightful administrators who used all the resources at their disposal to enact their visions. (p. 83)

For school leaders to create and sustain effective programs for ELs, including newcomer programs, it takes dedication and strong partnerships with community members and policy makers. In addition to having a student population who could benefit from this model, empathy and understanding about the unique needs of the students and the long-term benefits of such program models is imperative.

Scenario: Middle School Bilingual Program

Here is an example of an English language support program and the implications the different program characteristics might have for students. Table 2.2 is the schedule of a middle school EL enrolled in a bilingual program.

This school offers a bilingual model, English/Spanish, for ELs. The majority of the students are Spanish speakers who are enrolled in the program; these students primarily spend their day with each other in classes taught by teachers

Table 2.2 Sample EL Schedule

Block	Program	Courses
0		Homeroom
1	Bilingual	Math
2	Bilingual	Spanish Language Arts
3	ESL	Seventh grade ESL
4	Elective (Foreign Lang.)	Spanish
Lunch		
5	Bilingual	Science
6	Elective	Physical Education
7	Bilingual	Social Studies

who struggle with appropriately balancing both languages. Most of the teachers believe that bilingual education means instruction should be taught in the students' native language, in this case Spanish. The English instruction the students receive is during Block 3 (ESL) and Block 6 (Physical Education). This particular student chose Spanish as their foreign language elective. This course may or may not be different from Spanish Language Arts. Without a clear understanding of each course, the curriculum, and how the curriculum is implemented and assessed, it would be difficult for a principal to articulate to parents and stakeholders that students who are enrolled in this program have a balance of English and Spanish each day across all content area courses.

In addition to the primary language of instruction, there is the question of which language students will be assessed in. The language of test administration may be at the discretion of the teacher for informal assessments, but for state mandated assessments, there is a high probability that they will be administered to students in English.

For a student who is considered a newcomer, this model may provide the most access to content area courses. For students who have been identified as ELs since kindergarten, for example, how is this district's program model aligned to helping them becoming proficient in English? Outside of homeroom, lunch, ESL, and Physical Education, and based upon the teacher's understanding of bilingual education, it could be assumed the students spend the majority of their day in a Spanish-speaking environment. It is not simply a question of a "good" or "bad" program model but rather a question of whether the program model in place truly meets the needs of the students it serves.

Scenario: Elementary School Cluster Model

An elementary school has approximately 450 students with a small population of ELs (see Figure 2.1). This is the first year they have had newcomers in

Figure 2.1 Cluster Model in Elementary School

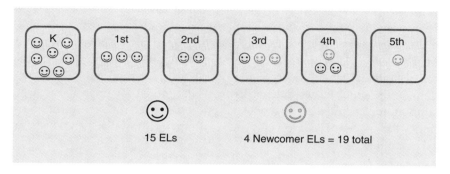

the upper elementary grades. They also have the largest number of enrolled kindergarten ELs they have ever had.

The population in this community is becoming more linguistically diverse. The school has an itinerant ESL teacher who provides one segment of ESL support for 50 minutes per day. The ELs are clustered in the same grade level classes. With the increase of kindergarteners and newcomers this year, pulling 19 ELs all together for language support is not the best approach. The ESL teacher has expressed her concern about her schedule to the principal and the ESL director for the district. If you were the principal at this school, what would you do to support the students, the general education teachers, and the ESL teacher? How might you and the ESL director work together to implement a better language support model?

Ultimately, program models need to be responsive to their student populations, regardless of how they were initially implemented. District and school leaders need to work together to assure that the program models in place are what the students need. To do that, programs must be properly evaluated. Evaluation of program models is an essential part of ensuring equity and access for ELs. In the scenario of the school featured in Figure 2.1, the principal was able to secure additional funding for a full-time paraprofessional who spoke Spanish.

The students then had a segment of ESL with their ESL teacher and a paraprofessional, thus lowering the student:teacher ratio. The paraprofessional also provided additional support to certain grade levels throughout the day and was able to work directly with the newcomers.

> Program models need to be responsive to student needs rather than reacting negatively to student enrollment trends

Assessing Program Models for Efficacy

A principal and I were discussing the daily 2-hour transitional bilingual program model in her school. She told me that "general education teachers don't really know what they do in there." This is often the case with language programs, because English language programs tend to operate in isolation. School-wide programs may or may not include the work of students who receive language services. For example, a school leader shared an upcoming afterschool event highlighting their Science, Technology, Engineering and Mathematics (STEM) initiatives. When asked about if and how the transitional bilingual model incorporated science and other related STEM standards, the school leader did not know. If the model for English language support implemented at the school is a pull-out model, then one must question what content ELs are being pulled from and how the ELs will have access to that content.

As described by Ward Singer and Staehr Fenner (2020, p. 68), program models must be designed by school leaders who can ask and answer the following questions:

1. Is our program designed in a way that ensures ELs' access to rigorous, grade-appropriate learning?

2. Is our program designed in a way that encourages ELs' integration with fluent speaking peers?

3. Are ELs scheduled in a way that is conducive to them receiving core content instruction and specials classes with peers?

These questions also lend themselves to assessing the efficacy of English language program models. As outlined in the "Dear Colleague Letter"

(U.S. Department of Justice & U.S. Department of Education, 2015), program models must

> evaluate the effectiveness of a school district's language assistance program(s) to ensure that EL students in each program acquire English proficiency and that each program was reasonably calculated to allow EL students to attain parity of participation in the standard instructional program within a reasonable period of time. (p. 9)

The guiding questions at the end of this chapter serve as guides to assist school leaders in evaluating their English language programs. To assess to what extent English language programs are meeting the needs of its students, school leaders must use multiple data sets (e.g., English language proficiency data, standardized tests, end of course exams); engage in dialogue around student achievement with teachers, parents, and stakeholders; and be prepared to make adjustments as necessary.

Staffing

There is no question that program models for ELs must be fully staffed with highly qualified teachers. The best planned English language programs cannot exist without teachers prepared to teach in them, principals prepared to evaluate the teachers who teach in them, and adequate teaching materials. Teacher shortages for ESL and bilingual programs are a nationwide concern. To combat this shortage, some teacher preparation programs are now embedding licensure to teach ELs within their degree programs. Some districts have programs to support bilingual paraprofessionals in becoming licensed teachers. Some districts recruit teachers from countries where the language is spoken by the majority of their EL population. These are just three examples of addressing the teacher shortage.

An analogy of these solutions to the teacher shortage problem would be if you had to decide to save a pool full of teachers who couldn't swim. Would you throw as many buoys as you could into the pool or would you quickly drain the pool? Draining the pool would be the best option. After draining the pool you'd teach them all how to swim and then fill the pool up again. An example of the *drain the pool* and *teach to swim* approach would be the 2015 statewide professional learning initiative educators in Massachusetts implemented in response to a U.S. Department of Justice finding that the state had not done enough to address the needs of its ELs. The Rethinking Equity and Teaching for English Language Learners initiative mandates a 45-hour structured English instruction course for general education teachers and a 15-hour course for school leaders (Espino Calderón & Slakk, 2020, p. 26). These courses are designed to help all educators be prepared for the linguistic and content needs of ELs in their schools. This statewide professional learning initiative also included policy changes because it affected teacher and administrator licensure. Now, state-wide, both preservice and in-service educators are better prepared to meet the needs of their students.

Professional Learning

Professional learning must encourage practitioner reflection and be ongoing and job-embedded in order to be effective. "Drive by" professional learning initiatives (solitary sessions with no follow up or follow through) and the like, as discussed in Chapter 4, may help districts meet certain requirements but rarely shift teacher practice enough to positively impact student outcomes. English language programs must be in direct alignment, as depicted in Figure 2.2, with core content area courses (standards based), while professional learning initiatives must be in direct support of curriculum and instruction *including* English language programs. Questions related to professional learning initiatives and EL achievement goals would require answers to *who*, *when*, and *how* the goals for each are strongly aligned.

If there is little to no alignment, then school leaders would need to reevaluate their current professional learning plans in order to be inclusive and proactive about the needs of ELs in their schools. More about professional learning, with a focus on ELs, is discussed in Chapter 4.

Figure 2.2 Unaligned School goals vs Aligned School Goals

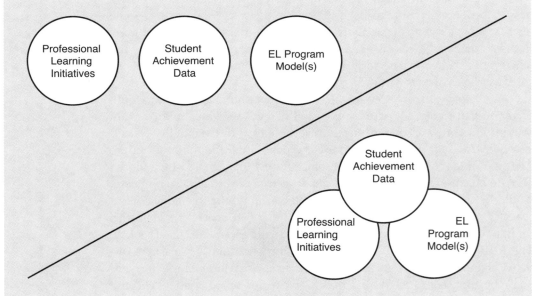

Communicating With Parents

Communicating and partnering with EL families are strongly connected to EL program models; parents and guardians must be well informed and part of the entire program process (identification, offering of support services, and eventually exiting). Language differences between school officials and linguistically diverse families bring additional challenges in regards to communication. These challenges are not impossible to address but take a commitment to inclusion and an effort to assure that supports are in place so that communication does not become or remain a barrier.

Schools have a responsibility to provide translation and interpretation services for all families who need it. The guidance is clear:

> SEAs [state education agencies] and LEAs [local education agencies] must provide language assistance to LEP [limited English proficient] parents effectively with appropriate, competent staff or appropriate and competent outside resources. To provide these services, LEAs may canvas staff to see if they are trained and qualified to provide effective language assistance, or obtain qualified interpreters and translators if staff is unqualified or if it would minimize the degree to which trained bilingual staff is called away from instruction and other duties to translate or interpret. Schools or LEAs may also use a language phone line to provide oral translation and interpretation services. Students, siblings, friends, and untrained staff members are not considered qualified translators or interpreters, even if they are bilingual. All interpreters and translators, including staff acting in this capacity, should be proficient in the target languages; have knowledge of specialized terms or concepts in both languages; and be trained in the role of an interpreter or translator, the ethics of interpreting and translating, and the need to maintain confidentiality. (U.S. Department of Education, 2016, p. 2)

It is not uncommon for school leaders to be unaware of these guidelines or to attempt to skirt them. The email requesting Spanish speakers in Figure 2.3 directly violates the preceding federal mandate in a number of ways.

The call for translators is informal and vague. People who respond, though they may have the best intentions, may not fit the federal criteria in the following ways:

- **Language proficiency:** Is their ability in the target language and English proficient? Do they know the specialized terms necessary in both languages?

- **Training:** Are they professionally trained to conduct interpretations? Did that training include ethics and issues of confidentiality?

- **Conflicts of interest:** Are they siblings or friends of students?

Figure 2.3 Email Requesting Spanish Speakers

Subject: Elementary School - Still Needs Your Help!!!

Date: October 7, 2019 at 11:47:58 AM EDT

Parent teacher conferences are fast approaching in ABC County. They will be next week on, **October 16-17.** XYZ Elementary school has a large percentage of families whose first language is Spanish. It is vital that teachers are able to communicate with parents about their children's academic progress. We need a good number of interpreters that can help us. **Please consider sharing your bilingual skills with us and/or feel free to share this message with your bilingual friends.**

These are the dates and times when XYZ Elementary needs interpreters:

Wednesday, October 16 - 12:30 - 7:30 PM

Thursday, October 17 - 8:00 AM - 7:30 PM

School leaders should be leery of practices such as this. Consult with district-level representatives to inquire about translation and interpretation services to assure laws are not inadvertently being broken.

Aside from the legal ramifications of the call for interpreters (Figure 2.3), there are ideological concerns as well. For example, asking for interpreters who can help make sure that "teachers are able to communicate with parents about their children's academic progress" is worded in a way that denotes

What Would You Do?

A high school has a population of ELs and offers a segment of Spanish Language Arts and Levels I and II ESL courses. Student achievement data show the cohort of ELs performing poorly in general education courses, especially in Math and Science. The teachers have also expressed concern about being able to effectively support ELs. The principal is working on a new professional learning plan for the next school year but had not thought much about the EL program model.

If you were the principal, how might you go about aligning professional learning goals with the current EL program model? How would you use results of EL student achievement data to support the professional learning initiatives, and how would you include that data? Who might you include in the planning and execution of the new professional learning plan?

_____

_____

_____

_____

 Available for download from **resources.corwin.com/justiceforels**

a one-way approach to parent communication. Parents should not attend parent–teacher conferences solely to receive information but rather to engage in receiving, sharing, and discussing information about their child's academic progress. Principals must also be aware of all languages represented in their schools in order to prepare for interpretation needs. Sometimes, resources are allocated to students speaking the most common second language: If a school has a significant population of Spanish speakers, then Spanish interpreters recruited. Smaller populations of other language speakers must be supported as well. If a school has families that speak Arabic, Vietnamese, and Portuguese, then interpreters for those languages may be needed as well. What is important to remember is that *all* languages matter!

Chapter 5, Partnering With Parents of ELs, goes deeper into the issues and importance of communicating and partnering with EL families.

When Parents Opt Out of Language Support Services

Parents or guardians have the right to opt out or waive their child's participation in a language support program. This may be a full or partial opt out. Often, decisions to opt out of language support can inadvertently cause educators to ignore the needs of ELs who are not directly receiving services. ELs may not be aware that, even if they've opted out of services, they are (still) identified as an EL—but their educators *must* be aware of this designation, because they are required to provide support to all students who are identified as EL, regardless of their participation in a language support program.

Why Parents Might Opt Out

Some reasons parents or guardians may opt out of services include the following:

- A staff member or another parent provides inaccurate information about the program models

- Scheduling conflicts with other classes

- Concern about the amount and quality of the work being assigned or missed if their child(ren) were to be pulled out for a segment of English language support

- A staff member explains to parents that certain classes (e.g., Bilingual Education) are full, encouraging opting out

- Concerns about programs offered are not fully explained or addressed

- Confusion between English language support and special education services

- Low confidence in the quality of the program models being offered
- Disagreement with school officials that their child(ren) need language support
- Disagreement with the philosophy of the program model being offered
- A decision to opt out for one school year is not revisited, and parents/guardians are not offered a chance to change their decision in subsequent school years
- Belief that once they decline services, they cannot request participation in the future

School leaders must be especially diligent in assuring that there is up-to-date documentation of parents or guardians who opt out of language support services for their child(ren). The decision must be voluntary, with the understanding that (1) their child will still participate in annual language assessment requirements and (2) their child's academic progress will still be monitored as required by federal law.

The federal mandate states, "school districts must provide guidance in a language parents can understand to ensure that parents understand their child's rights, the range of EL services that their child could receive, and the benefits of such services before voluntarily waiving them" (U.S. Department of Justice & U.S. Department of Education, 2015, p. 30). If parents or guardians do not fully understand what they are opting their child out of, this can be especially problematic.

Assuring parent understanding may require a number of intentional practices, such as having meetings with parents prior to program placement and having professional interpreters available. Program descriptions and related documents need to be provided to parents in a language they can understand. Professionally translated materials are imperative to ensuring parents understand what is being explained to them and the decisions they may be making.

Being Proactive for ELs Who Opt Out

School leaders should also be aware of the exact number of ELs who have opted out of services. If more students opt out of language support than opt in, there may be an underlying issue. For example, one middle school principal expressed her concern about the number of ELs who opted out of services in her school because of scheduling. Students wanted to participate in special courses and electives, such as band, orchestra, chorus, and technology. At this school, ESL block classes were scheduled for the same time as the majority of those special courses.

This is problematic for several reasons. First, students should not have to choose between a support they need to be academically successful and other courses they are interested in participating in. Second, this model is in direct violation of students' rights to not be unnecessarily segregated; they had to decide to take one necessary course over another optional course instead of being afforded the opportunity to participate in both.

Knowing how many ELs opt out of your support services is the first step in assessing what, if any, issues you might have with your programs. As stated in my blog, "Committed to Serve in 2020: Supporting ELs Who Opted Out" (Cooper, 2020):

> All decisions have implications. When a student opts out, what might it mean for their immediate language development, and what might it mean for their language acquisition down the line? When we understand the choices EL families have about what types of English programs being offered, we are in better positions to inform and support their decisions. (para. 10)

The next step would be acting upon the findings to assure no opportunities for improvement are inadvertently missed.

Long-Term ELs

An important reason school leaders should know why students are opting out of support programs is that the decision to opt out of language support services early leads to many students ending up as "long-term" ELs (LTELs), which can result in dire long-term implications for student achievement. Several definitions of LTELs exist, but scholars agree that, essentially, they are students

- in middle or high school,

- still identified as EL after several years (6+ years) of U.S. schooling, and

- unable to meet state-mandated exit criteria. (Menken & Kleyn, 2010; Olsen, 2010; Short, 2015; Thompson, 2015)

Short (2015) goes on to list additional characteristics of LTELs, including that they have strong oral language skills but difficulty in literacy. They may also have repeated grades (i.e., been retained), have interrupted schooling, be unmotivated to learn, and be at risk for dropping out of school. Keep in mind that no "profile" of LTELs exists and that various circumstances may be contributing to a student's status of LTEL. In Brooks's (2019) research on a mother's advocacy for her son who was identified as an LTEL, the mother explains all of the bureaucracy she experienced when trying to find answers to why her son, in middle school, was still taking an annual language assessment. He had initially been identified as an EL in kindergarten and was considered an LTEL by middle school. Imagine this mother's frustration: Her son's progress in attaining English was not clearly articulated regularly to her, from the time he was first identified until he reached middle school, and she wanted answers. There may be a number of variables associated with a student's status as an EL, LTEL, or dually identified EL—what is most important here is that systems and structures are in place with the best possible outcome for students and that their parents and guardians are a valuable part of what is happening in schools.

Bringing It All Together

The issues, examples described, and questions posed in this chapter affirm the importance that all school leaders be aware, knowledgeable, and supportive of the English language program models in their schools. School leaders must also work in tandem with school and district initiatives that are inclusive of culturally and linguistically diverse learners and their families. In order to do so, school leaders must commit to being *proactive* versus *reactive* to the ELs they serve and the educational experiences their schools are providing.

FOLLOW-UP QUESTIONS ....

1. What language programs are currently in place in your school?

2. Are all of the eligible students being served by this model? If not, why?

3. Are students that may have waived participation in the language support program being supported?

4. To what extent do the models avoid unnecessary segregation of ELs?

5. What evidence do you have that those programs are supporting positive student outcomes?

6. Considering your population of EL students, what, if any, language programs or revisions to language programs do you think are necessary in your school?

7. Is your language program fully staffed? If not, what steps might you take to fill those positions with highly qualified teachers?

8. Do your teachers have what they need in order for the language program model(s) to be successful?

9. How and how often are the goals and expected student outcomes of the language program in your school communicated with students, parents, and stakeholders (e.g., online, brochure, parent meeting/orientation)?

10. Once students reach proficiency in English, how are they being monitored?

FURTHER GUIDANCE AND SUPPORT RESOURCES ....

Bilingual Glossaries

- Bilingual Glossaries
  (research.steinhardt.nyu.edu/metrocenter/resources/glossaries)

- English/Spanish Education and Assessment Glossary
  (translationsunit.com/PDFS/2013_engspanglossary.pdf)

Blogs

- Committed to Serve in 2020: Supporting ELs Who Opt Out (blog.tesol.org
  /committed-to-serve-in-2020-supporting-els-who-opt-out/)

- Diversity ≠ Inclusion: Avoiding Segregative Practices With ELs (blog.tesol.org
  /diversity-%e2%89%a0-inclusion-avoiding-segregative-practices-with-els)

- Evaluation of Program Models for ELs: Let's Check and Reflect (blog.tesol
  .org/evaluation-of-program-models-for-els-lets-check-and-reflect)

- Instructional Program Models for Teaching English (www.empoweringells
  .com/instructional-program-models)

Program Evaluation Resources

- AIR English Language Learner District Curriculum Audit (www.air.org
  /project/curriculum-audits-districts-and-schools-english-language-learners)

- Challenges and Supports for English Language Learners in Bilingual
  Programs (ell.stanford.edu/sites/default/files/pdf/academic-papers/11-Brisk
  %20Bilingual%20Programs%20FINAL_0.pdf)

- U.S. Department of Civil Rights Developing Programs for English Language
  Learners (www2.ed.gov/about/offices/list/ocr/ell/programeval.html)

U.S. Program Model Statistics

- U.S. Department of Education Office of English Language Acquisition:
  English Learners and Instructional Programs (ncela.ed.gov/files/fast_facts
  /19-0353_Del4.4_InstructionalPrograms_122319_508.pdf)

- U.S. Department of Education Office of English Language Acquisition: Dual
  Language Learning Programs and English Learners (ncela.ed.gov/files/fast
  _facts/19-0389_Del4.4_DualLanguagePrograms_122319_508.pdf)

REFERENCES ....

Brooks, M. D. (2019). A mother's advocacy: Lessons for educators of long-term
  English learners. In H. Linville & J. Whiting (Eds.), *Advocacy in English
  language teaching and learning* (pp. 190–201). New York, NY: Routledge.

Cooper, A. (2020, January 7). *Committed to serve in 2020: Supporting ELs who opt out* [Blog post]. Retrieved from http://blog.tesol.org/committed-to-serve-in-2020-supporting-els-who-opt-out/

Espino Calderón, M., & Slakk, S. (2020). From language to language, literacy, and content. In M. Espino Calderon, M. G. Dove, D. Staehr Fenner, M. Gottlieb, A. Honigsfeld, T. Ward Singer,. . . D. Zacarian, *Breaking down the wall: Essential shifts for English learners' success* (pp. 111–133). Thousand Oaks, CA: Corwin Press.

Martin, M., & Suárez-Orozco, C. (2018). What it takes: Promising practices for immigrant origin adolescent newcomers. *Theory Into Practice, 57*(2), 82–90. doi:10.1080/00405841.2018.1425816

Menken, K., & Kleyn, T. (2010). The long-term impact of subtractive schooling in the educational experiences of secondary English language learners. *International Journal of Bilingual Education and Bilingualism, 13*(4), 399–417.

Olsen, L. (2010). *Reparable harm: Fulfilling the unkept promise of educational opportunity for California's long term English learners.* Long Beach, CA: Californians Together.

Short, D. (2015, April 27). *Long-term English learners: Blending academic language and content* (PowerPoint Slides). Retrieved from https://ncela.ed.gov/files/uploads/2015/Deborah_Short_LongTermELsBlendingAcademicLanguageandContent.pdf

Sugarman, J. (2018). *A matter of design: English learner program models in K–12 education.* Washington, DC: Migration Policy Institute.

Thompson, K. (2015). Questioning the long-term English learner label: How categorization can blind us to students' abilities. *Teachers College Record, 117,* 1–50.

U.S. Department of Education. (2016). *Chapter 10: Tools and resources for ensuring meaningful communication with limited English proficient parents.* Retrieved from https://www2.ed.gov/about/offices/list/oela/english-learner-toolkit/chap10.pdf

U.S. Department of Justice & U.S. Department of Education. (2015). *Dear colleague letter: English learner students and limited English proficient parents.* Retrieved from https://www2.ed.gov/about/offices/list/ocr/letters/colleague-el-201501.pdf

Ward Singer, T., & Staehr Fenner, D. (2020). From watering down to challenging. In M. Espino Calderon, M. G. Dove, D. Staehr Fenner, M. Gottlieb, A. Honigsfeld, T. Ward Singer, . . . D. Zacarian, *Breaking down the wall: Essential shifts for English learners' success* (pp. 47–71). Thousand Oaks, CA: Corwin Press.

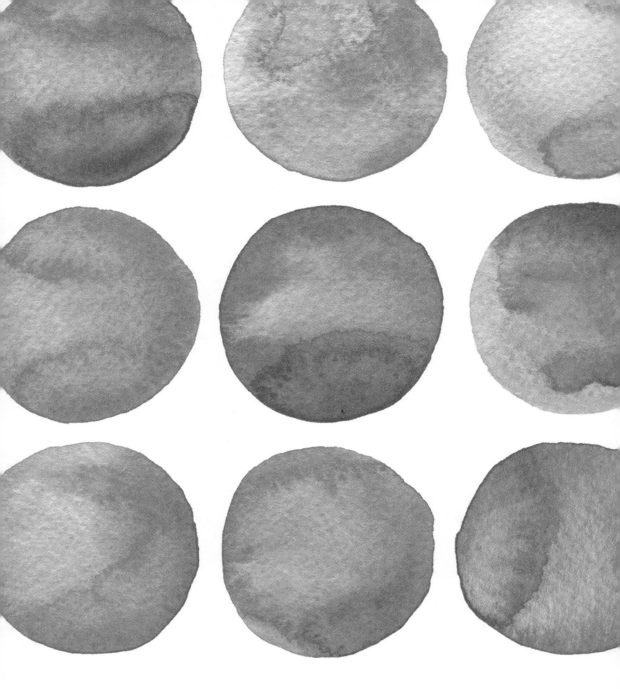

We need evaluation systems that are designed to support all teachers of English learners.

Evaluating Teachers of English Learners— Conversations Beyond the Rubric

Scenario: Needs improvement, Meets, Exceeds, or Not Applicable

An English as a second language (ESL) teacher teaches small groups of English learners (ELs) at an elementary school using the pull-out model. She teaches about six students at a time at a small, kidney-shaped table in the hallway. On the day she was formally evaluated, she taught a primary math lesson about number sense to a group of kindergarten ELs. By the conclusion of the lesson, she had used manipulatives, engaged students, and informally assessed them. Overall, she thought the lesson went well—until she received her written evaluation. She was extremely disappointed that she received a few areas that were marked as "needs improvement," including the area of planning and instruction regarding the lack of technology in her lesson. The school had a technology partnership with a company in the community. The partners had provided new SMARTboards in several of the classrooms and a set of Chromebooks for each grade level.

When I spoke to the teacher about her evaluation, she expressed her disappointment. I asked if she had requested a preevaluation meeting with her evaluator to discuss the rubric and to provide more context about her small groups. She had not. I asked if she expressed her concerns during the postevaluation. Again, she had not. She asked me, "What difference would it make now? I already received a Needs Improvement on my evaluation. I don't know what kind of technology I could use in the hallway. The Wi-Fi connection is really weak." I explained to her the value of being able to have those conversations *before* and *after* evaluations to provide the evaluator more context and to ask questions. An observation of a teaching lesson may not capture all of the nuances of the instructional practice nor fully capture the teaching and learning environment. Although the school leader who evaluated the ESL teacher had an expectation for technology to be part of instruction, this particular teacher needed specific support; she needed to know what that expectation might look like as part of small group instruction, in the hallway, at a kidney-shaped table with a low Wi-Fi connection.

Conversations Beyond the Rubric

Teacher evaluation remains a hot topic across the field of education. The words *evaluation* and *observation* alone can evoke stress and anxiety. As part of my teacher preparation program, I welcomed observations because they were framed around supporting me to become an effective practitioner. I remember eagerly planning lessons, finding resources that were standards based and of high interest to my students. I have fond memories of being supported by both my field experience supervisor and cooperating teacher. As a novice elementary school teacher, that experience was quite the opposite. Oftentimes, it felt like I was trying to do whatever they were looking for that would warrant a "good" rating—rather than what I thought I should be doing to improve student outcomes. Similar experiences have been had by other teachers. An instructional staff developer for equity and culturally relevant teaching told me,

> I feel like I really missed out on having a trusting working relationship with my evaluator/assistant principal and what that could have led to, as far as me growing in my teaching practice. My entire team always commented how they were fearful and anxiety-ridden when she came in to observe either formally or informally. (**Kimberly, personal communication, November 15, 2019**)

These kinds of experiences are unfortunate and unnecessary. As we work toward building teaching and learning communities with a spirit of collaboration, equity, and advocacy, we must change mindsets around teacher evaluation practices.

Evaluating ALL Teachers of English Learners and Students With Disabilities: Supporting Great Teaching (Staehr Fenner, Kozik, & Cooper, 2015), a book focused on K–12 teacher evaluation and diverse learners, was a pioneering text in ESL and special education. It outlines four principles necessary for equitable teacher evaluation practices for teachers of ELs and students with disabilities:

Principle 1: Committing to Equal Access for All Learners

Principle 2: Preparing to Support Diverse Learners

Principle 3: Reflective Teaching Using Evidence-Based Strategies

Principle 4: Building a Culture of Collaboration and Community

These four principles can be applied to various teacher evaluation systems and rubrics and embedded in conversations that support student achievement of diverse learners.

Principle 1 affirms the need for all educators to adhere to the laws and precedents that assure all students received full and equal access to public education. Evidence of Principle 1 could be both observable as part of instruction and action oriented as part of professional learning communities. Principle 2 focuses on how educators prepare to support the diverse learning needs of their students. This is primarily evident through how instruction is designed and executed. Pre- and postevaluation meetings are opportunities to converse about this principle. In some instances, pre- and/or postevaluation meetings are not required. If this is the case, I suggest educators of ELs request a meeting to avoid situations similar to what was expressed in the scenario described at the beginning of the chapter. Principle 3 elevates the teacher's ability to use evidence-based strategies for diverse learners. These strategies are concrete and observable but also take time to develop. This is where professional learning plans, individual and school wide (as discussed in Chapter 4), become necessary to assure teachers are prepared for diverse learners. Principle 4 highlights how communities of practice are built around inclusion of all stakeholders with a commitment to shared decision-making, sharing of resources, and cultivating a spirit of advocacy for diverse learners.

For educators of ELs, all of these principles must be embedded into teacher evaluation systems so that ELs and their teachers are fully included within teaching and learning communities. This requires work *beyond the rubric*.

Regardless of the adopted or created teacher evaluation systems and rubrics within a school, key understandings about diverse learning populations are necessary. *Evaluating ALL Teachers of English Learners and Students With Disabilities* calls attention to the importance of including the needs of diverse learners in teacher evaluation systems. Most teacher evaluation rubrics use phrases like *all learners* and *all students* so much so that the emphasis on *all* becomes watered down, and the unique needs of ELs are diluted into the needs of the masses so that they are no longer as distinct as they should be.

This chapter is designed to extend the ideas presented in *Evaluating ALL Teachers of English Learners and Students With Disabilities* by encouraging more conversation between teachers who teach ELs and teacher evaluators. The conversations that happen before and after informal and formal evaluations can help to build understanding about the students, the teacher, and the learning environment that simply cannot be captured by a single teacher evaluation document. Conversations beyond the rubric are what will ultimately serve as a bridge between evaluators and the teachers they evaluate with the goal of ensuring positive outcomes for all students—especially ELs. The federal guidance that addresses evaluation is vague when it comes to evaluating teachers of ELs. It simply states,

> SEAs and school districts that provide EL teacher training are also responsible for evaluating whether their training adequately prepares teachers to implement the EL program effectively. To meet this obligation, school districts need to ensure that administrators who evaluate the EL program staff are adequately trained to meaningfully evaluate whether EL teachers are appropriately employing the

training in the classroom and are adequately prepared to provide the instruction that will ensure that the EL program model successfully achieves its educational objectives. (U.S. Department of Justice & U.S. Department of Education, 2015, p. 15)

In order to truly support school leaders with their charge of evaluating EL teaching staff, we need to first ensure those leaders are properly trained to meaningfully conduct such evaluations. This affirms the importance of encouraging conversations beyond the rubric. In order to prepare for those conversations, all educators of ELs and their evaluators will need to first assess their understanding of the needs of ELs. They'll also need to assess teachers' access to resources that support best practices. Then, teachers will need to be prepared to articulate their needs to those who serve in leadership capacities (e.g., department heads, instructional coaches, leadership team members, or other teacher evaluators). These considerations are different, yet related, depending upon if you are the evaluator or the teacher being evaluated.

School Leaders Self-Assessment

For principals, it is important to know what to look for in classrooms with ELs, regardless of program model. I say this because I've been asked a number of times if teachers in EL programs should be evaluated by a different teacher evaluation rubric than general education teachers. That depends, but quite honestly, very rarely are school leaders able to completely change the teacher evaluation rubric prescribed by the district or state. Rather than changing the rubric, focus instead on what you *can* change: the conversations before and after observations. Guilamo (2020) agrees this is also true in bilingual and dual language classrooms:

The important point to understand is that if we are to have fair observations in bilingual and dual-language classrooms, we must have clear practices in place for observing effectively and accurately, regardless of the school-or districtwide adopted teacher evaluation framework. (p. 13)

Recently, I spoke with general education teachers with ELs in their classes about teacher evaluation systems. I asked them what they wanted their administrators to know about their ELs. Some of the responses included the following:

- My students' starting point, fluency in English, and overall ability
- Everything my EL students have had to overcome to be successful in school
- My students' backgrounds and their level(s) of proficiency
- How motivated and driven to succeed my EL students are

- My EL students have varying levels of both ability and confidence

- Students' amount of growth throughout the year, which can't be measured by one test

Such responses, which may not have been observable in classroom teaching, could easily be embedded into pre- and postobservation conversations. As part of a formal observation, administrators may see differentiation but are teachers able to articulate the reason for that differentiation? The *why* behind the strategies in place for ELs is just as (if not more) important than the *how*. For school leaders, statements like the preceding can be modified into questions that are more assets based. For example, an evaluator may ask the following:

- What would you like for me to know about the ELs in your class?

- Tell me about where your ELs are academically now and where they were earlier this year.

- What motivates your ELs? What are their strengths? Opportunities for growth?

- How are you using data to support their language and content development?

- What additional supports or resources do you need for your ELs?

Teachers of ELs Self-Assessment

When thinking about how teachers must self-reflect and assess their own needs in relation to preparing for ELs, Table 3.1 provides an example of how teachers can begin to express their needs through a series of reflective questions. This self-reflection is aligned to the professional learning needs assessment that is further described in Chapter 4.

Once data from self-reflections and self-assessments are gathered, school leaders have the entry points necessary to begin meeting the needs of their staff members. For example, if data meetings are planned, ensuring time and space to include English language proficiency (ELP) data would be important. Some administrators may believe the ELP data are for some teachers but not others, and this dangerous belief can further the divide between bilingual/ESL teachers and general education teachers that may already exist (Cooper, 2020). I encourage school leaders to both ask teachers how they are using ELP data to help differentiate instruction and also to help them articulate this use.

Look Fors: Key Considerations

I'm often asked what should be looked for when observing in classes with ELs—what specific strategies, compliances, or objectives, also known informally as "look fors." That depends. It would not be fair to say, "exactly what

Table 3.1 Teachers of English Learners Self-Assessment Checklist Example

Needs Assessments	Yes	No	Not Sure	Further Action Required
Do I know all of my students, especially those with diverse learning needs?	✓			
Do I have students who are identified as English learners? If so, how many?			✓	Need EL class information sheet. Email Ms. Amel
Do I have students who are identified as English learners and with an IEP? If so, how many?			✓	Not sure, IEP meetings next week.
Do I have or have access to all of the documents I need that tell me about my students (e.g., IEPs, home language surveys, registration forms)?			✓	Not sure I have all info needed.
Have I met and/or been in contact with the parents/guardians of my students?	✓			See notes from open house and email log.
Have I met with other teachers and/or support personnel who provide services to my students with diverse learning needs?		✓		Service model meetings 2x per semester are planned.
Do I plan regularly with other teachers and/or support personnel who provide services to my students with diverse learning needs?		✓		Create schedule to co-plan w/ Mr. Hendrix for this semester.
Am I aware of and do I regularly implement appropriate strategies that allow my students access to the content being taught?			✓	Working on this—need to implement informal assessments—follow-up on PD plan due soon!
Do I regularly use accommodations based on my student's learning needs?	✓			
Do I understand the additional assessments my students take?		✓		Need to get an update.
Do I use the data from various assessments to help plan instruction for my students?		✓		Need to get an update

Source: Adapted from Staehr Fenner, D., Kozik, P., and Cooper, A. (2015).

IEP = individual education plan; PD = professional development.

 Available for download from **resources.corwin.com/justiceforels**

you look for in all classes," nor would it be realistic (or reasonable) to have a 20-page detailed list of look fors. Following are some nonnegotiable look fors that can be applied to any evaluation, observation rubric, or checklist, in both formal and informal classroom visits:

- standards-based lessons
- four domains of language (SWRL: speaking, writing, reading, and listening)
- defining common language
- motivating students

Standards-Based Lessons: Content and Language

There is no question about the value of language and content being taught simultaneously: Language proficiency and content knowledge are developed in tandem. Regardless of the content and language standards used by your state, lessons must be standards based because ELs will be assessed for both their level of ELP and for their academic performance on state-mandated assessments required by the Every Student Succeeds Act (2015). The challenge in effective evaluation is related to how each individual interprets teaching to the standards. Are most teachers in your school aware of the language standards adopted by your district? If not, how might that information be shared as part of professional learning? (See Chapter 2 for ideas.)

Essentially, all teachers teach language—hence the need for knowledge of content and language standards. As affirmed by Slakk and Calderón (2020), "[The Every Student Succeeds Act] expects that ELs and their peers will receive a well-rounded education based on college and career readiness standards" (p. 25). Awareness of and application of both content and language standards are part of creating and sustaining a shared sense of responsibility for EL achievement. It's up to school leaders to determine the extent to which both content and language standards are being addressed. Because of the aforementioned challenge related to the interpretation of standards, this determination is not necessarily easy to make and relies heavily on how content and language standards are embedded as part of ongoing professional learning. Links to classroom instruction videos with ELs are provided in the resource list. These videos are helpful examples of what content and language instruction could look like. They can be viewed as part of professional learning communities or individually while offering some insight into a variety of grade levels, content areas, and ELs at varying levels of proficiency.

Four Domains of Language

The four domains of language are speaking, writing, reading, and listening. The acronym I use to help educators be more cognizant of language is SWRL, though it lists the domains in an order atypical of how second language acquisition usually happens. (Typically, ELs acquire language in this order: listening, speaking, reading, and then writing; however, the acronym works because it helps teachers to become aware of and remember the domains, and this awareness is most important.) Building awareness around language, at its core, is essential for assuring linguistic equity.

In a recent professional learning session, I surveyed a group of high school educators about language, specifically the four domains, as part of instruction. The question was "Which domain of language is exercised the most in your class?" Overwhelmingly, listening was the response. Speaking was exercised the least, which was surprising because encouraging student discourse using strategies such as "turn and talk" has been a widely accepted practice as part of incorporating strategies for ELs into teaching. The teachers reported that reading and writing were assessed far more than speaking and listening, which was even more surprising, because it conveyed a direct disconnect between assessment and teaching practices, at least based on teacher perception.

SWRL is not to be used as a form of English imperialism but rather a form of linguistic empowerment; both the first *and* second languages are important in second language acquisition. Two major research studies affirmed the importance of reading and writing skills in first and second languages for ELs' success in school. Findings from the research conducted by The National Literacy Panel on Language-Minority Children and Youth and the National Center for Research on Education, Diversity & Excellence included the following:

- Second language literacy development is interrelated with a number of variables (e.g., first language literacy, second language oracy, socioeconomic status).

- Oracy and literacy can develop simultaneously.

Certain first language skills and abilities transfer to English literacy, phonemic awareness, comprehension and language learning strategies, and first- and second-language oral knowledge (August & Shanahan, 2006).

In any program model, students can be encouraged to use and held accountable for using all four domains of language in the target language and, if appropriate, in their native language. "Assuring ELLs speak, write, read, and listen every day will require intentional teaching. The process of becoming intentional practitioners who develop both content and language will be different for everyone but necessary for all students to be academically successful" (Cooper, 2013, p. 56). Figure 3.1 is an example of one teacher's exit ticket after a professional learning workshop. Figure 3.2 is a photo of a poster a teacher made for her classroom after attending a professional learning workshop I designed and facilitated.

Figure 3.1 Teacher Feedback After Professional Learning
Focused on Language

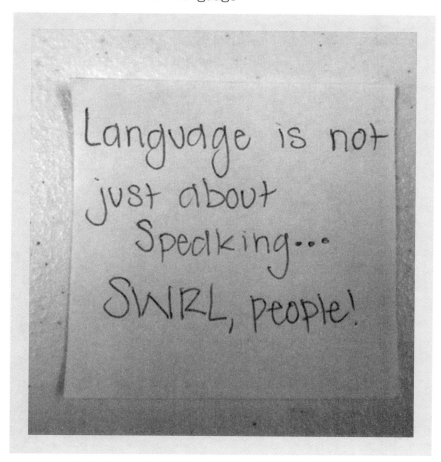

Defining Common Language: *Best Practices* and *Academic Language*

Defining common language is an important part of teacher evaluation systems and structures. There are a lot of terms, acronyms, and phrases specific to teaching and learning. Sometimes, defining this lexicon can be challenging because it can be difficult to agree on meanings. Terms like *academic language* and *best practices* can lead to misunderstandings and misinterpretations. As part of preobservation meetings and professional learning communities, clarify these terms so that all parties are in agreement.

What do we mean when we talk about best practices, for ELs specifically? It is impossible to recognize and observe something that has no definition. Zacarian (2018) writes,

> While the term best practice is highly used, we have to think about
> it as a way of teaching that has been found to be promising when we

Figure 3.2 High School Teacher's SWRL Poster

Source: Teresa Butcher

use our own professional craft to make it work based on what we know about our particular students (their personal, cultural, social, and world experiences), our classroom environment, and the goals of any unit of study that we teach. *(para. 5)*

I prefer the phrase *intentional teaching* to *best practices*. There are a number of definitions of intentional teaching. I define intentional teaching as "being able to justify the 'what' and 'how' of what is taught and expected from students at various levels of English language proficiency" (Cooper, n.d.).

Academic language is another common phrase that needs to be defined and clarified. There are a number of definitions of academic language that exist, but they all have commonalities. Problems arise when teaching vocabulary in isolation—which is part of academic language—gets confused for teaching academic language. For example, when observing instruction, either formally or informally, do you hear students using academic language? That depends upon how you define it. If you ask different teachers to define academic language, chances are you'll hear slightly different definitions. The goal here is to go beyond the definition to what happens in classrooms with ELs. Are students using the language of the content? Are they answering in complete sentences? Do they engage in discourse with their peers and teachers? I encourage school communities to come to a consensus around academic language and its use in classrooms by all students but especially ELs. Without defining common language, we run the risk of leaving these concepts up to our own interpretation versus having a shared understanding.

Motivating ELs

There are a number of researchers who affirm the importance of motivation as part of language learning. Dörnyei has researched language learner and language teacher motivation for decades. Why is this important? "Without sufficient motivation, even individuals with the most remarkable abilities cannot accomplish long-term goals; nor are appropriate curricula and good teaching enough to ensure student achievement on their own" (Dörnyei, 2018, p. 1). Though school leaders and teachers are responsible for creating and sustaining equitable learning environments, they cannot guarantee all learners will be highly motivated. They can, however, create the expectation that learning is meaningful and requires learning engagement. To support learner motivation and autonomy, teachers should ensure that students can articulate why they are learning what they are learning and why this new knowledge is important to them. There are many ways to motivate ELs, including

- interest surveys,
- learning style inventories,
- student choice in assignments and informal assessments, and
- student goal-setting journals.

Aside from formal grades, using portfolios and regularly acknowledging effort and growth can be part of second language learning expectations that increase learner motivation.

Articulating Needs to Support ELs

How can we ask teachers to teach harder, reach all learners, differentiate instruction, use culturally responsive pedagogy, and be in tune with and responsive to students' social-emotional learning needs when we (e.g., school districts and other educators) have not provided teachers with all they need to know about the students they serve? Sometimes, we don't know what we don't know. If teachers are better informed about their students, they'll have a clearer idea of what kinds of questions to ask about student needs. Time and opportunity to begin the work of self-assessment and collaboration can lead to a more focused teaching direction with clearer outcomes for teachers and their students (see Tables 3.1 [p. 60] and 3.2, which present educator and evaluator self-assessment examples). For teachers to know *who* is an EL in their class alone is not enough, but it is a start. Once teachers know more about their ELs—and when they have school leaders who can help to support their depth of knowledge around those ELs—they can truly begin articulating both their needs and their students' needs.

Table 3.2 Teacher and Instructional Coaches Checklist

Teacher	Yes	No	Comment	Coach	Yes	No	Comment
1. Do I show respect for my coach as an instructional leader?				1. Did I show respect for the teacher's expertise?			
2. Did I ask for help brainstorming ways to address challenges?		•		2. Did I help the teacher brainstorm ways to address a challenge?			
3. Did I know my ELs' levels of English language proficiency?				3. Did I know the levels of English proficiency of the ELs in this class?			
4. Did I highlight both strengths and weaknesses of my ELs?				4. Did I highlight a strengths perspective of EL?			
5. Did I ask for additional support to collaborate?				5. Did I offer support for current and future collaboration?			
6. Did I articulate my vision of EL student success in my class?				6. Did I learn about the teacher's vision for shared responsibility of ELs?			
7. Did I articulate my understanding of the suitability of the lesson for ELs?				7. Did I increase my understanding of the suitability of the lesson for ELs?			

Teacher	Yes	No	Comment	Coach	Yes	No	Comment
8. Did I ask for additional resources to support ELs in my class?				8. Did I suggest additional resources to support ELs?			

Source: Cooper & Staehr Fenner, 2016

Sometimes, even when teachers really know their students, they still need help articulating what they need from their evaluators, and, sometimes, they just don't know what they need. The same is true of administrators. Too often, EL pedagogy gets dismissed as "just good teaching," so opportunities to truly acknowledge and celebrate intentional teaching are missed. This is where pre- and postevaluation conversations can be beneficial: Both parties can discuss what they know, what they need to know, and what they expect—and gaps can be identified and discussed. Those gaps are crucial because they correlate directly to gaps in instruction, pedagogy, and student needs.

Supporting Preservice Teachers

When I teach preservice content area teachers about teaching ELs, the conversations we have at the beginning of the semester are quite different from those toward the end of it. After spending time out in their field placements, the preservice teachers often express their further interest in the ELs they support and concern for some of what they observe. They are developing as teacher advocates, and it is a joy to be part of! I had one preservice teacher share how excited she was to learn one of her students spoke Swahili, exclaiming, "I didn't know he was an EL!" And another preservice teacher wondered about the amount of time an EL spent on the computer instead of part of whole group lessons.

Preservice teacher educator Dr. M. Williams outlines opportunities to embed social justice practices as part of preservice teacher education requirements. New teachers must be advocates for themselves and for the linguistically diverse learners they serve. The sooner they begin understanding advocacy issues, the easier it becomes to continue those practices as part of their careers. Table 3.3 shows some of the situations that preservice teachers will have to navigate in order to become self- and student advocates.

Table 3.3 Preservice Teacher Preparation for Advocacy

Situations	Reflection Questions	Possible Opportunities for Action
Mandated Curricula Many school districts have content curricula that teachers must use. Creators of these may or may not have integrated social justice strands.	• What are some opportunities to integrate social justice? • How may I prompt students to think critically about the content? • How can I "disrupt" the current narrative?	• Social justice "overlay" for lessons/units (begin planning early) • Search for ways to incorporate other perspectives.
Planning Meetings Planning meetings are integral components of any successful educational program. During the week, teachers may participate in several meetings, such as: • Grade Level • Leadership • MTSS/RtI/IEP • Faculty/Staff	• Do conversations focus on what students "can't do" or do they highlight what students "can do" with support? • Are stereotypes presented during conversations?	• Be prepared. Come to meetings with "something to offer." Develop the reputation of being ready/armed with valuable input. • Know your data! • Be prepared to offer a "maybe, but have you thought about..." • Offer a positive perspective or factors that may have impacted a negative situation.

Situations	Reflection Questions	Possible Opportunities for Action
Data Talks Data analysis is a critical activity that should guide school-wide planning and classroom instruction.	• Do conversations focus on students' failures or shortcomings (not reaching established targets)? • Do conversations highlight students' growth? • Do conversations highlight students' potential?	• Ensure that language development data are reviewed in addition to content achievement data—if ELs do not learn language, they will not learn content. An analysis of language development data should begin any conversation about ELs' progress. • Offer suggestions to build on students' strengths. • Highlight students' growth. • Share ways to develop a culturally and linguistically responsive approach to RtI for ELs.
Advocating for ELs Many states have professional standards that focus on teachers as advocates for their students. Advocacy is a way to operationalize social justice.	Instances in which students may need a teacher advocate: • Student may have chronic absences. • Student may be failing a course. • Student may struggle with planning and organizing.	• Schedule meetings with parents. • Schedule meetings with students. • Have practical suggestions ready to assist students.

(M. Williams, personal communication, July 6, 2019)

EL = English learner; IEP = individual education plan; MTSS = multitier system of supports; RtI = response to intervention

When school leaders hire new teachers, conversations around becoming part of a new culturally and linguistically diverse learning community are imperative. Not all preservice teachers have the same experience and preparation for teaching ELs. It's important to gauge new teachers' understanding and awareness of three dimensions—process, medium, and goals: "The process of learning a second language, the role of language and culture as a medium in teaching and learning, and the need to set explicit linguistic and cultural goals" (de Jong & Harper, 2005, p. 118). These supports should be embedded into any new teacher mentorship programs so that being mindful and responsive to EL needs become the expectation early on in one's career.

Conversations around how ELs are assigned to classes are necessary. For example, it is unfortunate yet not surprising that in some schools,

A middle school principal has to evaluate the teachers who teach in the bilingual program at her school. The school leader does not consider herself bilingual but knows a few words and phrases in Spanish. She visits the bilingual program classroom often and knows all of the students by name. To effectively conduct a formal observation, what tools or resources does she need so she can provide constructive praise and feedback for the lesson she'll observe? What might the preobservation meeting look and sound like in preparation for the observation?

_____

_____

_____

_____

 Available for download from **resources.corwin.com/justiceforels**

new teachers, those with minimal to no training to teach ELs, are assigned to teach ELs. This is sometimes the case even when other teachers in the same grade level have licensure, training, and more experience teaching ELs. Scheduling can be laborious yet tantamount to expected outcomes for ELs.

School leaders who are responsible for evaluating teachers who teach in bilingual and/or dual language programs in their schools must take creative measures to fairly and effectively evaluate the teacher. This may include using video, audio recording, interpreters, and transcripts of classroom discourse, assignments, and assessments. What is not explicitly stated in the scenario, yet paramount to linguistic equity, is the relationship between the principal and the teacher. How might their relationship contribute to the evaluation process? A relationship built around collegiality, professionalism, and mutual respect is undoubtedly one that can contribute to greater outcomes for students.

Bringing It All Together

This chapter highlights a number of related issues around equitable teacher evaluation practices. It is not a question of one rubric over another—rubrics may be beyond one's immediate control. Equitable teacher evaluation practices are built upon engaging in conversations beyond the rubric that affirm intentional teaching, address predetermined look fors, and ensure teachers can articulate their own needs and those of their students.

Include your list of nonnegotiable look fors that might not be captured in evaluation systems. What are the must-haves that you as the school leader expect to be authentically embedded as part of instruction and assessment? They need to be made clear for all teachers in your school, but especially those who are teaching ELs. Being able to support teacher development with a focus on linguistic equity, regardless of the prescribed teacher evaluation systems, can lead to school leaders feeling (and being) informed and empowered.

FOLLOW-UP QUESTIONS ....

1. Are educators in your school participating in pre- and postobservation meetings?
   a. If not, how can those meetings add value to existing practices?
   b. If so, how are those meetings being used to highlight the needs of ELs?
   c. Are protocols needed to help facilitate conversations in these meetings to highlight ELs?

2. To what degree are your prescribed teacher evaluation systems inclusive of ELs?

3. How can the needs of ELs be elevated as part of teacher evaluation systems?

4. How do you support self-reflection and self-assessment as part of teacher practice to prepare for ELs?

5. How are all domains of language embedded in teaching and evaluation practices?

6. What types of questions can be included in pre and postobservation meetings that are in support of EL achievement?

7. How are teachers being supported as they become more culturally responsive and equitable practitioners?

8. Are teachers comfortable articulating their needs and instructional practices as they relate to EL achievement?

9. Are all teachers able to analyze English language proficiency data?

10. Are your professional learning plans inclusive of ELs' needs and in alignment with your teacher evaluation systems? If not, what additions can you make to existing plans to include evaluation considerations for teachers of ELs?

FURTHER GUIDANCE AND SUPPORT RESOURCES ....

Additional Readings

- AIR Promoting Success for Teachers of English Learners Through Structured Observations (www.air.org/project/promoting-success-teachers-english-learners-through-structured-observations)

- Ohio Teacher Evaluation Pre-Post Questions (education.ohio.gov/getattachment/Topics/Teaching/Educator-Evaluation-System/Ohio-s-Teacher-Evaluation-System/Teacher-Performance-Ratings/Pre-and-Post-Conference-Sample-Questions111015.pdf.aspx?lang=en-US)

Videos of Instruction

- Andy Mizzell, Academic Vocabulary Development (wida.wisc.edu/resources/academic-vocabulary-development)

- Colorado Practical Ideas for Evaluating General Education Teachers of Bilingual Learners (www.cde.state.co.us/educatoreffectiveness/practicalideaguidebilingual)

- Colorín Colorado Classroom Videos (www.colorincolorado.org/videos/classroom-video)

- Jeff Zwiers's communication-based and interactive learning (www.jeffzwiers.org/videos)

- Teaching Channel Videos (https://learn.teachingchannel.com/videos; select English Language Learners for "Topic")

REFERENCES ....

August, D., & Shanahan, T. (Eds.). (2006). *Developing literacy in second-language learners: A report of the National Literacy Panel on language-minority children and youth*. Mahwah, NJ: Lawrence Erlbaum Associates.

Cooper, A. (n.d.). *Using writing prompts with ELLs: My summer vacation (part 3)*. Retrieved from https://www.colorincolorado.org/blog/using-writing-prompts-ells-my-summer-vacation-part-3#comment-553

Cooper, A. (2013). Putting Action 13 into practice. In M. Gottlieb, *Essential actions: A handbook for implementing WIDA's framework for English language development standards* (pp. 56–57). Madison, WI: Board of Regents of the University of Wisconsin System.

Cooper, A. (2020, March 3). *Evaluation of program models for ELs: Let's check and reflect [Blog post]*. Retrieved from http://blog.tesol.org/evaluation-of-program-models-for-els-lets-check-and-reflect

de Jong, E. J., & Harper, C. A. (2005). Preparing mainstream teachers for English language learners: Is being a good teacher good enough? *Teacher Education Quarterly, 32*(2), 101–124.

Dörnyei, Z. (2018). Motivating students and teachers. In J. I. Liontas (Ed.), *The TESOL encyclopedia of English language teaching* (Vol. 7, pp. 4293–4299). Alexandria, VA: TESOL.

Every Student Succeeds Act of 2015, Pub. L. 114–95, §1177 (2015)

Guilamo, A. (2020). *Coaching teachers in bilingual and dual-language classrooms: A responsive cycle for observation and feedback.* Bloomington, IN: Solution Tree Press.

Slakk, S., & Calderón, M. (2020). From compliance to excellence. In M. G. Dove, D. S. Fenner, M. Gottlieb, A. Honigsfeld, T. W. Singer, S. Slakk, . . . D. Zacarian, *Breaking down the wall; Essential shifts for English learners' success* (pp. 21–45). Thousand Oaks, CA: Corwin Press.

Staehr Fenner, D., & Cooper, A. (2016, April 4). *Inclusive teacher evaluation for all educators of ELLs.* Paper presented at TESOL International Association PreK 12 Day, Baltimore Convention Center, Baltimore, MD. This looks like the beginning of a new citation. Staehr Fenner, Kosik & Cooper should go on the next line.

Staehr Fenner, D., Kozik, P., & Cooper, A. (2015). *Evaluating ALL teachers of English learners and students with disabilities: Supporting great teaching.* Thousand Oaks, CA: Corwin Press.

U.S. Department of Justice & U.S. Department of Education. (2015). *Dear colleague letter: English learner students and limited English proficient parents.* Retrieved from https://www2.ed.gov/about/offices/list/ocr/letters/colleague -el-201501.pdf

Zacarian, D. (2018, May 22). *What education buzz words are most overused? [Blog post].* Retrieved from https://zacarianconsulting.com/2018/05/22/what -education-buzzwords-are-the-most-overused/

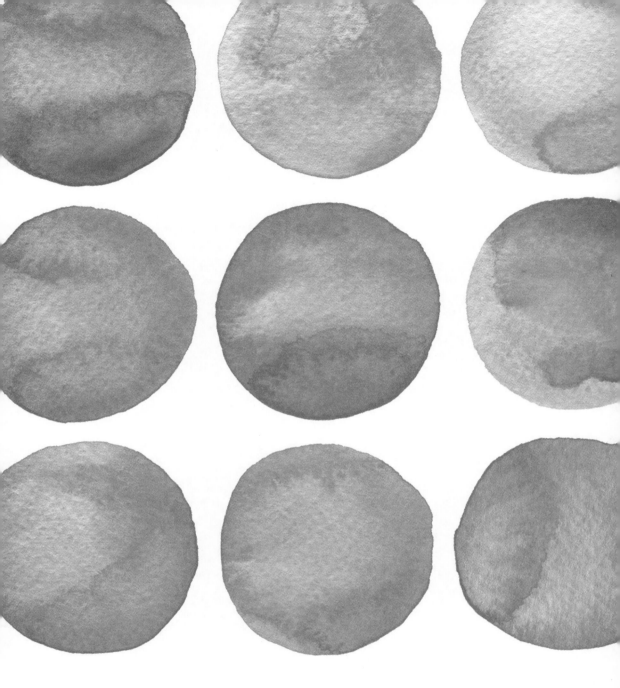

*No more drive by professional learning,
pop-up professional learning, or random acts
of professional learning*

Action Steps for Job-Embedded Professional Learning With a Focus on English Learners

Scenario: A Program by Any Other Name Is Not the Same

A high school with a number of English learners (ELs) offered a sheltered instruction courses for their students. The courses consisted of English, Science, Social Studies, and Mathematics. The students' levels of English proficiency ranged from beginner to advanced. When I asked the team of approximately 10 sheltered instruction teachers about any sheltered instruction training they'd had, here were three of their responses:

Teacher A: What sheltered instruction training? When?

Teacher B: I think I have the book.

Teacher C: I went to a training a long time ago.

This is an excerpt from a real conversation I had with teachers. When I asked them what, specifically, about their program made it sheltered, each teacher had a slightly different vision of what "sheltered instruction" meant and what it should look like from an instructional standpoint. As described in Chapter 2 (Table 2.1), sheltered instruction is a model where content courses are taught by teachers who have been trained to differentiate instruction so that ELs have access to content concepts while developing academic language proficiency in English.

Regardless of what title is given to an English language program, professional learning (PL) must be specific to the needs of the students and to the program model(s) in place. Teachers must be prepared to teach students in a well-defined and highly functioning program model—one that is deliberate and intentional. Through further conversation with this group of high school teachers, it became evident that the program model title was just that, a title. I wondered if they had assumed it was a sheltered instruction program because it had always been referred to that way. How did their differing visions about the sheltered instruction model affect the learning environment and learning outcomes of their students? If there is no clear understanding and consensus of the program model and how it is beneficial for its learners, ultimately, student learning and outcomes may not be consistent with the expectations.

I suggested the teachers work on developing their vision of their EL program and a mission for how students would be supported throughout their educational careers. I prompted them to ask themselves questions, such as

- How will students be supported outside of sheltered courses?

- What do general education teachers know about ELs and the sheltered instruction model?

- Is there fluidity so that students will eventually transition into general education courses?

These questions, which were directed both at the teachers and at the school leaders, encouraged the team to think strategically about the students that they taught and their program model. Answers to questions like these are absolutely necessary to truly support ELs, though they can be complex and layered.

PL for teachers of ELs is a civil rights issue. This is especially important to embed PL that is inclusive of existing program models and includes all staff members who teach in those program models. In regards to staffing and supporting EL programs, the federal guidance states,

> School districts have an obligation to provide the personnel and resources necessary to effectively implement their chosen EL programs. This obligation includes having highly qualified teachers to provide language assistance services, trained administrators who can evaluate these teachers, and adequate and appropriate materials for the EL programs. (U.S. Department of Justice & U.S. Department of Education, 2015, p. 14)

How can we ask educators of ELs to teach harder, reach all learners, be culturally responsive practitioners, use data to drive instruction, and teach the "whole" child without providing them with all of the information and resources they need to be able to do so.

A PL Cycle of Inquiry

How do we define and engage in PL with a focus on ELs? This chapter uses the term *professional learning* rather than *professional development*, *teacher training*, *workshops*, or the like. Guskey (2000) defines PL as "those processes and activities designed to enhance the professional knowledge, skills, and attitudes of educators so that they might in turn, improve the learning of students" (p. 16). PL is the process by which educators define and/or identify an issue, strategize a plan of action, implement the plan, assess the results, and repeat the process. This process does not happen in isolation. Although educators may engage in independent learning, they may also engage in PL as part of a community, most commonly referred to as a professional learning community (PLC). Key purposes for PLCs include improving pedagogical knowledge (how and what we teach) and improving academic outcomes for students.

As part of their PLC+ framework with the goal of planning and implementing key purposes, Fisher, Frey, Almarode, Flories, and Nagel (2020) ask five key questions:

1. Where are we going?

2. Where are we now?

3. How do we move learning forward?

4. What did we learn today?

5. Who benefited and who did not benefit?

Answering these questions with ELs in mind is the foundation for engaging in PLCs that are intentional, collaborative, results driven, and equitable. Let's take a close look at the cycle of inquiry and how it supports PL and PLCs. Figure 4.1 illustrates this process, which is referred to as the "cycle of inquiry."

PL must be effective, enabling educators to develop the knowledge and skills they need to address students' learning challenges, and there must be evidence for that effectiveness. To be effective, PL requires thoughtful planning followed by careful implementation with feedback (Mizell, 2010,

Figure 4.1 Cycle of Inquiry

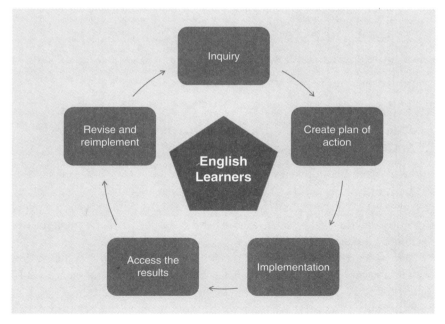

p. 10). The cycle of inquiry in Figure 4.1 provides an illustration of the steps involved in the PL process. The target demographic must be at the center of the cycle—in this case, ELs.

PL Action Steps

PL to build capacity is a critical need (Zacarian, 2011, p. 83). In order to start and sustain PL conversations around ELs in your school, PL conversations must be ongoing, documented, and results oriented. PL is not a one-time or annual event. It is cyclical in nature and adaptive to the needs of its participants. A common issue with PL related to English language teaching is that objectives are repeated without an intentional focus on either linguistic growth or designing a diverse approach that meets the needs of linguistically diverse learners. School leaders must evaluate their PL community structures and design them to be more inclusive of ELs. This chapter outlines action steps for school leaders to help sustain EL academic achievement through long-term, job-embedded PL.

Although a number of PL models exist, including instructional coaching, book studies, and use of independent consultants or companies to facilitate PL, this chapter provides a lens to those approaches that highlight the needs of ELs. A one-size-fits-all approach is not prescribed or suggested; each school has its own unique demographics, cultures, climates, and set of needs.

The following action steps are explained in this chapter:

- Preparing an EL PL needs assessment

- Evaluating past and ongoing PL as it relates to ELs

- Custom designing PL based on the needs assessment

- Applying flexibility to adjust PL goals and outcomes as needed

- Creating options for sustainability

Preparing an English Learner Professional Learning Needs Assessment

In the research I conducted for my dissertation, PL specifically designed for teaching ELs correlated to teachers' higher sense of perceived self-efficacy (Cooper, 2009). PL matters! The more specific to the population of students being taught, the better. Even more specific than student populations are data about those students.

The most frequent comment I receive when asked to provide PL is, "We need strategies." I ask clients about their English language proficiency (ELP) data and past PL practices. Quite often they have had very little training that includes ELP data analysis and very little training that focuses on English language teaching strategies or best practices in general. Often, schools collect and analyze formal and informal data about student performance, but there is no mention of ELs and no inclusion of ELP or development data. Without this critical information, data-driven discussions will never be complete (Cooper, 2015, p. 254). Jackson (2016) states, "Do very little without data. One of the most powerful reasons for using data is to plan Professional Development" (p. 12).

Asking the right questions

Recently, I spoke at a 2-day conference, and the lack of data usage for PL was evident. Although both days featured sessions that focused on ELs, neither session specifically addressed using English proficiency data. Close analysis of such data should not only be used, it should drive PL and pedagogy. When this happens, requests for PL become more specific and, therefore, useful:

- "We need PL to help our ELs become better writers."
- "How can we enhance strategies like 'Turn and Talk' to develop academic discourse?"
- "How can you help us analyze our data so that we use intentional strategies with our ELs?"

The more specific the questions, the more specific answers can be.

A PL needs assessment requires research and questions that help educators understand where the school community is currently at in terms of EL achievement, where they need to be regarding preparedness for teaching ELs, and how they can begin to reach those goals. The following is a list of sample questions that can be used as part of a needs assessment.

English Learner Professional Learning Needs Assessment Sample Questions

1. How much PL have we had with a focus on ELs? (List number of sessions, dates, and expected outcomes.)

2. How is PL aligned to our school initiatives?

3. Based upon our school initiatives, what types of PL are being requested by our staff with regards to ELs?

4. Which staff members have been included in the PL? (Include support staff members such as paraprofessionals.)

5. What type of PL schedule/service model is preferred by the staff members? (E.g., do they prefer PL facilitated by PL communities? Specific grade-level planning days/times? Teacher workdays? Staff meetings? Online learning? Individual coaching? Attendance at state and national conferences?)

 Available for download from **resources.corwin.com/justiceforels**

How should school leaders answer these questions? What if they are not able to answer them at all? What if these questions lead to additional questions? Good!

First, acknowledge that developing a PL needs assessment is a process. This process involves the goal of improving outcomes for all students, but especially ELs. Prioritizing these questions, organizing them into subcategories, or using a checklist to track your progress leads to important data to support PL initiatives.

To illustrate what the process may look like, consider example School A (see Chapter 1), where both kindergarten and first grade have the highest number of ELs. Paraprofessionals are scheduled to support students in these grades. They rotate their schedules so that they are attending to kindergarten in the morning and first grade in the afternoon. By answering Question 4, "Which staff members have been included in the PL?", and including support staff members, school leaders would know if they need to build in PL for EL support personnel if their paraprofessionals hadn't previously been part of the plan. Regarding Question 5, "What type of PL schedule/service model is preferred by the staff members?," school leaders may need an individualized approach. District- or school-wide PL time might be scheduled by a central office, and the PL model may be different from what teachers prefer if given the choice. A school leader could administer a survey to inquire about PL preferences. The data collected from that survey would be used to address the current PL offerings, the model through which it is offered, and to whom the PL is offered. For example, educators could commit to administering the PL in small groups during their on-site grade-level planning meetings versus something offered for larger groups of teachers at the central or district office. By having a macro to micro perspective of supporting students, school leaders can not only see the gaps but also support educators of ELs in diverse ways.

During a recent discussion with a district leader, we looked over an upcoming curriculum planning summer project. As I read the outline, I noticed phrases such as *academic vocabulary*, *content and language objectives*, *use of strategies*, and *academic achievement*. I believed it was necessary for me to know more about the district's understanding and definition of these concepts for two reasons. First, this would help me determine if the district needed specific support before undergoing a new curriculum plan. Second, this information would assist the district leader in developing a differentiated PL. To this end, I asked the district leader the following questions:

- Have the teachers previously had PL on understanding and incorporating content and language objectives?

- If not, what will that training consist of? If so, what were the outcomes?

- Do you have any examples of content and language objectives for teachers to reference?

- What is the expectation for writing, creating, posting, and demonstrating content and language objectives as part of a lesson?

- What do you mean by *academic vocabulary*? Does that include *academic language*? (Academic vocabulary refers to isolated words typically associated with content concepts—for example, *glaciers*, *global warming*, *atmosphere*. Academic language is the discourse expected of students—for example, the number of spoken words and the amount of written text.) If so, how can we deepen understanding of these concepts?

- I'm not seeing where ELP has been included in this curriculum plan. Where might ELP data analysis be incorporated?

These questions helped the district leader to look beyond initial PL plans that may have missed with the opportunity to build participants' backgrounds in certain areas. Another example of differentiated PL is learning that is created as a direct response to a PL needs assessment. One district hosted a 2-day PL summer institute. Over half of the participants reported that they did not know how to analyze ELP data, which they needed to know how to do before they could learn new teaching strategies. Part of learning how to analyze data includes disaggregating the data, during which process participants would identify trends and target potential areas of support.

Using an annual ELP assessment, the ACCESS for ELLs 2.0, as an example (Figure 4.2), here is what one K–8 school's ELP data may look like:

Figure 4.2 Sample English Language Proficiency Assessment: Total Number of Students Assessed

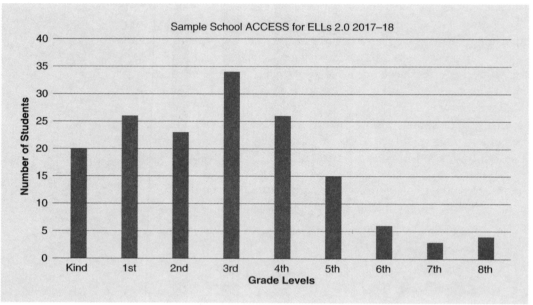

From this example, we see that the most ELs are in Grades K–4. Would grade levels with a significantly lower number of ELs need the same PL as grade levels with a significantly higher population? Not necessarily. A more intensive focus may be implemented in Grades K–4, while a more individualized approach could be utilized for Grades 6–8. Either way, analysis of ELP data must be done annually, at the minimum. If not, as cohorts of students move from one grade to another, their teachers may not be prepared.

The graph in Figure 4.3 shows the students' overall proficiency levels in English. Level 1 is the lowest level and Level 6 is the highest. Educators can look for student performance trends and areas in need of specific attention by looking at the data this way. From this example, we see the majority of the kindergarten students are at Levels 1 and 2, while the majority of Grade 4 students are at Level 3. These considerations will need to be part of planning, implementation, and sustaining PL for both K and 4th grade teachers.

The next step would be to disaggregate the data by language domain and plan instructional strategies around the areas in need of development. By studying the data from their state's annual ELP assessment (i.e., the ACCESS for ELLs 2.0), teachers were able to ask deeper questions about their students' academic ability.

Figure 4.3 Proficiency Level Across Grade Levels

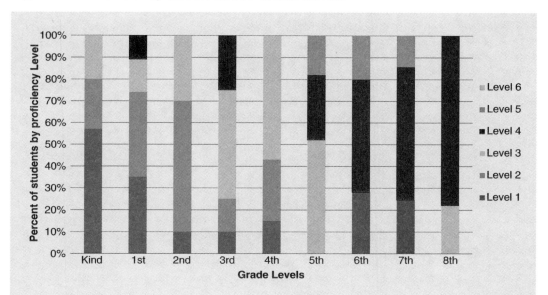

Understanding the data and what they could mean

Teachers may be presented with any amount of data, but they must be able to dissect it. This means understanding the format of how the ELP data are presented. Are the data presented quantitatively, narratively, or both? Depending upon how the data are presented, the format may have to be revised in order to be communicated to various audiences (e.g., school board members, teachers, parents, and students). Following are some data points that bear consideration.

- *The number of grade levels that have the highest number of ELs.* This information helps to focus on grade levels that may need more support than others. If the majority of the population is in a few grade levels, then conversations have to be centered around the needs of those learners and their teachers.

- *The levels of proficiency across all grade levels.* Understanding ELP and grade-level expectations (e.g., standards and assessments imperative to the charge of differentiating instruction) is imperative if teachers are going to be able to effectively differentiate instruction for ELs.

- *Students who reached proficiency according to their state/district exit criteria.* How are students who have reached proficiency being supported? What does proficiency look like for different learners at different ages and stages? For example, the language needs for a student to be successful in second grade are different than the language needs for a student to be successful in seventh grade. Although there are similarities, there are clear differences as well. Once a student has reached proficiency in English in their grade level, are supports still necessary? If so, to what extent and what do those supports look like?

- *Students who were close to reaching proficiency according to their state/district exit criteria.* The "close to" subgroup evokes several questions. These questions may include matters such as how close the students were to exiting, the program model that provides language support, and the specific areas that are showing the most need). Once school leaders and teachers take a closer look at this particular group, they can begin to strategize the most effective ways to support the ELs. If we aggregate them back into the population of ELs, we miss the opportunity to celebrate their academic growth and achievement.

- *Number of students per grade level and/or proficiency level.* This issue is linked to one of the previous issues. Understanding the English language varies by proficiency, grade level standards, and expectations. The number of students per grade level and per proficiency level affects the PL different teachers should receive. If teachers are expected to differentiate instruction, then the expectation should be that PL must be differentiated as well. Adjusting PL plans to meet the needs of students and their teachers is imperative for ongoing student achievement.

To return to my earlier example (Figure 4.3) and question, "Would grade level(s) with a significantly lower number of ELs need the same PL as grade levels with a significantly higher population?", the answer may depend upon students' levels of proficiency and the needs of their teachers. If the number of students at lower levels of proficiency is significantly higher (let's say 60% of the school's overall EL population), then the PL designed should focus on strategies appropriate for students at that particular level and beyond.

Generally speaking, teachers participate in a number of PL sessions with a focus on improving teaching strategies for all students. However, teachers often struggle with adjusting those strategies specifically for the ELs they teach. The question is how teachers can differentiate instruction for both content and language development. For example, teachers may be encouraged to use graphic organizers to help support content concepts. Conversely, using a blank Venn diagram would not be the best language scaffold for a student at a lower level of proficiency without additional supports. Nor would solely partnering ELs who speak the same native language as the only support those students would receive as part of their instruction. These are examples of differentiation but not differentiation intentionally designed for the various levels of ELs that may be taught.

By thinking about the aforementioned considerations as part of a PL needs assessment, school leaders can begin to design PL with a focus on ELs that is in direct response to their staff needs. Although these questions could be used with any student population in mind, the goal here is to continue highlighting and supporting the needs of ELs and the teachers who teach them. The needs assessment could also serve as evidence of how the school has developed in terms of meeting the needs of its linguistically diverse learners.

Evaluating Past and Ongoing Professional Learning as It Relates to ELs

Evaluation of learning is a crucial part of PL in general. All too often, teachers from various schools are required to attend a particular PL event or session; they attend and leave, without any follow-up or expectations for implementation. These kinds of sessions are sometimes referred to as "drive-by PL," "pop-up PL," and "random act of PL." Without follow-up, the PL that is most often implemented misses what the teachers of linguistically diverse learners need. If a school implements a writing-across-the-curriculum initiative, for example, with a limited number of sessions, without including aspects of second language acquisition as part of PL, then the initiative would inadvertently ignore the needs of ELs. This would leave teachers with the responsibility to scaffold writing instruction for ELs without the depth of knowledge they would need to do so.

In some cases, PL plans have no follow-up because they have been stopped, perhaps due to funding or a change in leadership, only to be reimplemented years later. One instance that comes to my mind is a small school district in the southeast United States that contracted me in 2015 to facilitate a 1-day workshop for its English to Speakers of Other Languages (ESOL) team. I designed and facilitated the workshop for the district. In 2018, after a change in district leadership, I was contacted again for PL. I met with the EL program coordinator and members of the district leadership team to discuss both their short- and long-term plans regarding supporting ELs. The absence of PL specific to their EL population since 2015 for both the ESOL team and general education teachers was concerning, especially because their EL population had increased. I worked with the district to arrange ongoing PL support. The district leaders agreed and understood the importance of inclusive, ongoing, job-embedded, and population-specific PL, and they are now moving forward with these PL plans.

In the preceding example, the school district had no follow-up for their original PL plans because the plans themselves fell through. In most cases, however, the PL plans are carried out—and still lack the critical evaluation component. Guskey (2000) asserts the five critical levels of professional development evaluation:

Source: Guskey, 2000, p. 82

How districts rate or evaluate their PL varies, but a great strategy for making the evaluation effective is backward design. This is similar to designing classroom lesson or activities: Think about the goals and objectives first. School leaders should consider what they want teachers to know and do as a result of the PL. The short term is easiest to plan, and the long term can be challenging. Additionally, school leaders should look back at previous PL practices to determine what was missing. Once that data are readily available, they can cross analyze or triangulate the results of the PL with student achievement results to begin the process of custom designing and moving forward with a new PL plan.

Custom Designing Professional Learning Based on the Needs Assessment

Once school leaders have data from their PL needs assessment, they can begin to customize PL for their schools; customization is necessary to close achievement gaps between ELs and native-English-speaking students. The following is a quote from a district leader who recognizes the importance of connecting PL to student achievement goals:

> When I became Federal Programs Director in 2014 I knew I needed help with understanding our EL population. It was through the help of a consultant who specialized in ELs that my role as a district leader became more transparent and effective. I now have a better understanding of how to use English language proficiency data to support district and school initiatives. For example, through conducting walkthroughs we were able to identify instructional practices that directly supported both content and language development. We have had to customize ours because historically the annual English language proficiency assessment was administered and forgotten. We now study the data and make instructional decisions based on our ELs [sic] level of English proficiency. Our administrators can now talk

about this data and their EL population with knowledge and understanding. This is important because our state is adding EL proficiency to our school and district report cards. Working with a consultant has allowed us to become familiar with this assessment and the resources available for teachers. Our conversations have become more specific around helping ELs succeed. In the district strategic plan, under Goal 1, which is, "Foster student excellence and academic achievement with a curriculum that recognizes our cultural diversity," we include making sure our curriculum content utilizes the cultures, languages, and histories of our diverse students while expanding our professional development for teachers to be able to accomplish these goals. **(A. Ashby, personal communication, July 17, 2018)**

The district leader highlights how the use of ELP data had not been utilized in the past, which created a clear sense of urgency for a new PL plan. This district needed PL from the top down in order to build their capacity to better serve ELs. In supporting districts with top down PL, a macro to micro approach must be applied. This means a leveled approach to the "who" and "how" of PL with a focus on ELs. Figure 4.4 shows the individuals immediately impacted by this district's new PL plan, which focused on analyzing ELP data.

The first-year PL plan includes district and school leaders and teachers. This is represented by those inside the box. As they begin to embed this PL as part of their ongoing development, they can create more learning opportunities for additional educators, paraprofessionals, front office staff, guidance counselors, and others who support ELs through indirect instruction. This is represented by those inside the black box. The specific PL needs as they relate to ELs may be different for those with different roles throughout the district and school, but it is just as important and necessary for those who directly teach ELs.

Culturally responsive pedagogy

The needs assessment may show, as we've seen, that ELP analysis and instructional strategies are required, and that the learning should begin with the district leadership and trickle down to the classroom educators. It could, however, show that there is a need for culturally responsive pedagogy. In the following example, an educator explains how districts must create and embed PL that is reflective of the needs of its students and school community in general:

Many times districts require educators to participate in professional learning that does not align with the instructional needs of students nor of educators. In addition to core curriculum, professional development opportunities for educators who work in diverse learning environments, *educators* should engage in some form of cultural awareness professional development. As Dr. Beverly Daniel Tatum states, "Sometimes the assumptions we make about others come not from what we have seen on television or in books but rather from what

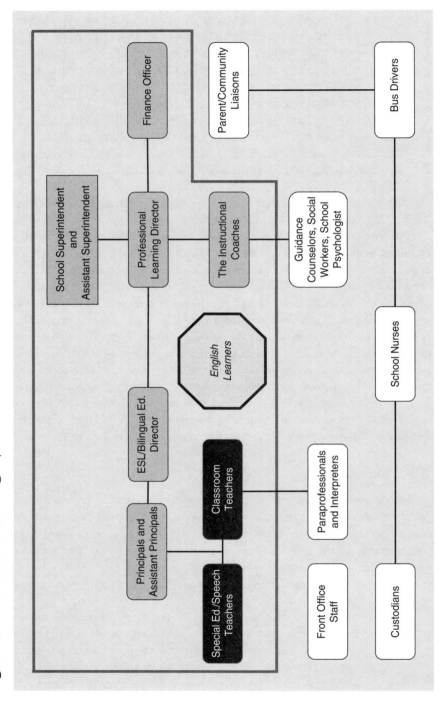

Figure 4.4 Professional Learning Impact

we have not been told." As school leaders take a proactive approach to teaching and learning, it requires them to take an active, intentional journey of creating unbiased opportunities for students to learn. Many of the textbooks are outdated and lack images or experiences that reflect the current demographic of students that we are educating. As we move forward in 21st century learning, we must create and participate in professional learning that is not biased, culturally aware, and relevant. (**C. Austin, personal communication, July 20, 2018**)

Part of culturally aware education is incorporating language teaching into PL. The school leader must have an asset-based perspective of his or her EL population, viewing the diversity of their thoughts, cultures, and values as a strength. To this end, the school leader must have a fundamental understanding of language, cultural diversity, social justice, and nonbiased practices. Following is an example of how such an asset-based approach and fundamental understanding can (or should) come into play for developing an EL program.

In preparation for sustaining a Navajo heritage language program model, the coordinator, Dr. Begay (2018), describes the need for differentiated PL for the teachers:

> You cannot just speak Navajo—you must be trained in the foundation of the methodologies and theories. Since summer 2017, the language teachers have received intensive training that has resulted in a significant paradigm shift. Professional development and learning was led by consultants from the Indigenous Language Institute and the University of New Mexico's American Indian Language Policy Research and Teacher Training Center.

In this case, the school leader recognized that she alone could not have an asset-based approach and fundamental understanding of the EL population's culture—for true access to a high-quality education, all of the educators needed to take this approach and have this understanding.

PL for support staff as needed

PL with a focus on ELs must extend beyond teachers and administrators. Curtis (2008) states, "The simplest way to do this is to incorporate everyone in the language teaching organization into the professional development plans" (p. 123).

It is easiest to consider PL for those who directly instruct ELs (classroom teachers, English as a second language (ESL) teachers, etc.), but it is just as important to consider those who support ELs outside of the classroom. School attendance officers, for example, are an imperative part of supporting student achievement. Generally speaking, their focus is to reduce absenteeism rates. Because student achievement is correlated with attendance, school attendance officers can play a vital role in helping reduce absenteeism for ELs.

In one school district in which I offered PL, the attendance officers were neither aware of how students were identified as ELs nor aware of the assessments those students were required to take. As the attendance officers attended the PL, they learned who was identified in their school as ELs, whether any of these students had high absenteeism rates, and basic information about their state's ELP assessment (e.g., when the test was administered, the components of the assessment, and the implications of how students perform). Students who have high absenteeism are at risk for a number of academic and social emotional issues. After the PL, these staff members were better prepared to support the entire school community, including ELs, with an increased level of awareness of assessments administered by the district.

The aforementioned example shows how school leaders should customize PL in order to fully meet the needs of the linguistically diverse learners and those who teach them. PL options can span the gamut: They can be very specific (e.g., using ELP data) or more general and holistic (e.g., understanding multiculturalism). They can directly instruct the classroom teachers of ELs or they can train other staff who indirectly support ELs. It is important to utilize the PL needs assessment to determine exactly what kind of PL your school needs.

Support for individual teachers as needed

Just as with students, at times teachers also need differentiated support. This is true for a number of reasons, including the overall competency of the individual a teacher, the curriculum and standards being used, and the needs of the students being taught. When individual teachers need support, instructional coaching is an appropriate option if available.

Instructional coaches, especially those with in-depth of knowledge of supporting ELs, are a huge benefit to learning communities. Instructional coaches are there to support teachers and are not formal evaluators. Through a collaborative approach, instructional coaches and teachers create plans to develop instructional practices to improve student outcomes. Instructional coaches typically work across content areas, including supporting EL teachers, which requires a specific set of skills. Figure 4.5 represents how the school leaders may lead the PL charge while instructional coaches have their "boots to the ground" when it comes to assuring those PL objectives are being implemented with fidelity.

Figure 4.5 also shows how instructional coaches may provide support to both ESL and general education teachers, both populations that teach ELs through various program models.

In many cases, PL with a focus on ELs is facilitated for teachers and instructional coaches simultaneously. Although this may be the most economical approach, the needs of instructional coaches and teachers can be vastly different. In some instances, instructional coaches do not have in-depth of knowledge about second language acquisition or strategies that support both language and content development. In these cases, instructional

Figure 4.5 Professional Learning Plan

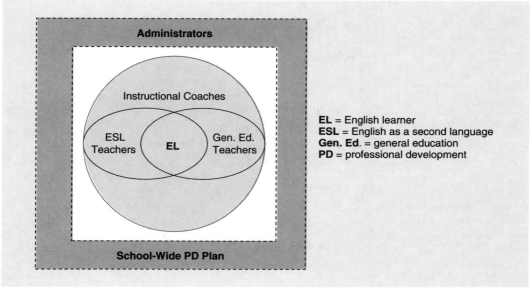

Available for download from **resources.corwin.com/justiceforels**

coaches would need their own customized PL before they could be charged with supporting other teachers of ELs.

For example, if an instructional coach has a background in literacy, should a school leader make the assumption that this professional is prepared to coach teachers of ELs in literacy and developing academic language? Not necessarily. Literacy education is primarily focused on native English speakers. Using English as the foundation prepares teachers for monolingual English speakers. The literacy needs of ELs who are receiving academic language instruction but may not be literate in their native language present a different challenge for their teachers. In situations such as these, we need customized PL for the instructional coaches. Lastly, instructional coaches themselves may have a wealth of experience working in diverse school communities, but school leaders cannot assume that they are well equipped to coach teachers with second language acquisition, academic language, and the like.

Applying Flexibility to Adjust PL Goals and Outcomes as Needed

Darling-Hammond, Hyler, and Gardner (2017) explain that for professional development to be effective, it must include specific necessary parts. Effective PL

- is content focused;
- incorporates active learning utilizing adult learning theory;

- supports collaboration, typically in job-embedded contexts;

- uses models and modeling of effective practice;

- provides coaching and expert support;

- offers opportunities for feedback and reflection; and

- is of sustained duration.

I believe flexibility is missing from this list. Being flexible is important because it allows for areas of adjustment or refinement. Many factors can affect even the best-laid PL plans, including teacher attrition and changing EL demographics within a school. For example, a school community may suddenly receive ELs from an area impacted by a natural disaster. Consider the aftermath of Hurricane Maria in 2017. Thousands of Puerto Ricans—more than 27,000—poured into Florida afterward (Dobrin, 2017). A Florida school's existing PL plan would likely have been insufficient because it may not have included understanding the social-emotional needs of traumatized students.

Additionally, PL plans that do not allow for adjustments can leave participants trying to piece together gaps in their knowledge and the goal(s) of the PL. A flexible PL plan might include the development of a PL community (PLC) or options for independent learning. Online courses and book studies can be options as well, because they offer more flexibility in choice and time. Offering multiple options, however, does not mean discord. Independent or individualized portions of a PL plan must include protocols and documentation, such as a form or log. Keeping track of differentiated PL is important for continuing to support the overall PL plan. For example, this process may involve setting the goal(s) of an individualized PL plan, creating a narrative of why this approach is best, compiling a list of artifacts and resources to be used or collected, and outlining outcomes and proposed next steps.

Let's take writing for example. If a teacher is teaching her third grade students how to write a persuasive essay, but she has an EL who is considered a newcomer, then mainstream writing workshops for PL will not help her meet the needs of all of her students. This teacher would benefit from learning about supporting second language acquisition through writing, specifically for newcomers. By implementing individualized PL, teachers can focus on the learning needs of specific learners in a way that may or may not be addressed by district-wide PL. In short, school leaders and teachers who are aware of and responsive to any outliers within their ELs population—and who allow for the same responsiveness in their PL plans—will have greater success around student achievement initiatives.

I was recently facilitating a PL session where a teacher told me she was just two weeks away from earning her TESOL endorsement. She was excited and looking forward to completing the program. However, as I talked to her, I quickly realized she was not well versed in analyzing ELP data. I asked her if analyzing data was part of her graduate level coursework.

Although she responded "No," she mentioned she was glad she was now receiving this training in my PL session. This situation highlights a PL need for the district's program leader. If other teachers had completed the same or a similar endorsement program but it did not include analyzing ELP data, a plan to meet and discuss the course content would be necessary. Being flexible about what learning opportunities are needed and how to best meet those needs is necessary for school communities that serve ELs.

Creating Options for Sustainability

Long-term funding is a major concern for sustaining initiatives as they relate to ELs. How can school leaders sustain an initiative that supports linguistically diverse learners specifically at his or her school, particularly if the funding is inconsistent from year to year? How can we avoid the "one and done" approach to PL?

To begin with, when it comes to funding, a strong partnership with the district's PL coordinator, who is responsible for PL budgets and financing, is extremely beneficial. If these district leaders have a solid understanding of the needs of the learners within your school, they are better informed when it comes to supporting your PL initiatives. A PL coordinator could help to extend your PL plan beyond the "one and done" approach by helping you explore options for using both Title III and Title II A funds. Partnering with institutes of higher education and state departments of education for teacher preparedness initiatives may be an option to consider as well.

When funding is uncertain (or minimal), there are still other options for sustainable PL.

Student shadowing

A creative way to sustain PL with a focus on ELs is to engage in a student shadowing approach. Soto-Hinman's (2010) research on preparing teachers for ELs describes student shadowing as

> a technique for examining specific areas of an [ELs] school experience and gaining insight into the student's perspective about school. Shadowing involves the selection of a student (often at random) and following him/her for 2-3 hours, noting classroom and campus activities. The purpose of student shadowing is to gather information about the daily life of an [EL] student in order to participate in a larger conversation on improving the educational experiences of students. (p. 3)

Ultimately, the objective for teachers who participate in student shadowing is to view learning experiences from their student's perspective. Not only are the teachers observing an EL's academic behavior, they are also noting how the student is interacting with his or her learning environment.

The observation of student listening and oral engagement contributes to the sense of urgency for intentional practitioners. It also provides additional thoughts about teaching students and also a new approach to advocating for them. Observing the student's view and the instruction provided are both powerful learning experiences that lead to the question of whether these experiences are part of perpetuating problems or facilitating solutions (Soto-Hinman, 2010, p. 6).

Common planning time

Another way to sustain PL that can be directly controlled by school leaders is the use of common planning time. Common planning time between ESL teachers and content teachers affords them the opportunity to plan and support ELs throughout units of study. Honigsfeld and Dove (2012) define the importance of collaborative planning as "instructional collaborative activities that allow a teacher to align teaching objectives, materials, learning strategies, and assessment so that [ELs] can be supported in a cohesive manner" (p. 42). Time to plan is necessary if we are going devote the necessary attention to the needs of ELs on a consistent basis as part of school improvement efforts.

Instructional and peer-to-peer coaching

Instructional coaching is an option as well, assuming coaches have an in-depth of knowledge about the academic needs of ELs or specialize in teaching ELs. Without this specific skill set, coaching lacks the specificity needed to help teachers become intentional practitioners of ELs.

Peer-to-peer coaching is an option that would support teachers learning together in a smaller setting. Alford and Niño (2011) state, "Peer coaching is a non-evaluative way for teachers to observe and learn from each other" (p. 71). Trust, transparency, and the willingness to accept constructive feedback are essential components of any coaching model.

Independent consultants and PL organizations

By partnering with independent consultants who provide PL or organizations that specifically address the needs of ELs, the needs of the school and how to best address those needs can be differentiated. This approach can be beneficial for the school leader who may have a specific area that needs to be addressed and allows for more flexibility with services provided. This could include on-site support as well as research, virtual coaching, and project management off-site. What makes this a sustainable option is that consultants can help build capacity over shorter periods of time and in particular focus areas. Table 4.1 shows a sampling of nationwide organizations that offer PL for educators of ELs.

All of these options for sustainable PL, and a few others, are outlined in Table 4.2. Remember that the list is not exhaustive, nor does it suggest

Table 4.1 Organizations That Provide Professional Learning for Educators of ELs

Organization	Description of Select Services Related to Professional Learning
CAL (Center for Applied Linguistics) cal.org	A nonprofit organization that supports diversity, equity, and access for linguistically diverse learners. They offer professional development institutes that focus on specific needs of school communities (e.g., teaching reading, teaching newcomers, and language assessment).
CARLA (Center for Advanced Research on Language Acquisition) carla.umn.edu	Professional learning for second language educators is offered through an annual summer institute, international conferences, and local and regional seminars. Some options include workshops on heritage language programs, teaching language online, and creating language assessments.
NABE (National Association of Bilingual Education) www.nabe.org	A nonprofit professional organization that offers membership and professional support to educators of bilingual/multilingual students. They offer an annual conference, symposiums, and an advocacy institute.
TESOL International Association www.tesol.org	A nonprofit professional organization that offers professional learning through an annual convention, online courses, workshops, and publications. Worldwide symposiums and workshops to support educators of English learners from early learners through adulthood.
The Instructional Coaching Group www.instructionalcoaching.com	This organization offers professional learning for educators who serve as instructional coaches. Although they do not specifically focus on educators of English learners, the institute provides an in-depth study of the instructional coaching cycle.
WestEd www.wested.org	Offers options for English language program model development and evaluation, including the dual language model. They provide overall program models and technical assistance and offer an annual summer institute.
WIDA www.wida.us	A consortium of states that use the same standards and assessments for English learners. They offer professional learning for members, state departments of education, and individual schools. Some of their topics include differentiation for linguistically diverse students and purposeful lesson planning.

one model over another. The options can be used in tandem or in isolation, depending upon the needs of the school.

Regardless of the model(s) chosen, consider the short- and long-term goal(s) of a PL plan and how they—the goals, and not just the plan itself—will be sustained. For example, one district offers ongoing, yearlong PL on sheltered instructional practices for ELs. Because this is offered by the district at the school level, PL is sustained by incorporating discussions about sheltered instruction as part of grade-level planning meetings. Teachers are

Table 4.2 Options for Sustainable Professional Learning

Types of Sustainable Professional Learning	Description	Considerations
EL Student Shadowing	Participants observe ELs in classroom settings. Documentation of instruction and EL engagement are used to evaluate one's perspective and instruction. (Soto-Hinman, 2010)	The number of ELs within a school and a feasible schedule to allow for release time for observer. Protocols may be used so that observations and data collection are uniform.
Collaborative Planning Time	ESL teachers and general education teachers are afforded time to plan collaborative lessons and assessments for ELs. (Honigsfeld & Dove, 2012)	The number of ELs and ESL teachers, grade-level distribution of ELs, and units of study to plan for must be taken into consideration when scheduling time for planning. Will planning time be allotted regularly? If so, how often and for what time frame? For example, once per 8-week unit for 30 minutes a day or weekly for 45 minutes during grade-level planning time?
Peer-to-Peer Coaching	Participants conduct peer classroom observations. Informal feedback is provided on a specific area(s) of focus, usually determined by the teacher being observed. Pre- and postobservation meetings are conducted as part of the process.	Nonbiased feedback is key to establishing a positive coaching relationship. Clear goals and outcomes that improve practice is the central focus. Additional support may be needed to learn how to use coaching protocols or observation rubrics.
EL Instructional Coaching	An instructional coach works with a teacher or group of teachers of ELs. Coaching strategies are intentionally designed to include and assess all domains of language.	Coaches must have an in-depth of knowledge about first and second language acquisition, cultural diversity, social justice, and nonbiased pedagogy.
Independent Study	Participants self-design and research an area of focus depending on the needs of their ELs. This may involve online learning, graduate level coursework, and attendance at local or national conferences.	School leaders should keep abreast of their staff members' progress if using this approach. For example, if additional degrees or licenses are obtained as a result of independent studies, school leaders should make note of such additions regarding teacher credentials.
EL Educator Consultants	Differentiated professional learning with the ability to directly support school leaders and teachers across short- or long-term projects.	Finding and partnering with those who specialize in the specific areas in need of support, budgeting, and outlining the scope of work are required.

EL = English learner, ESL = English as a second language

able to plan and collaborate on a number of sheltered instructional practices in small groups with a focus on the learners in their grade level. In this case, the sustainability relies on a twofold partnership. The district provides training on sheltered instruction while the school leader and his or her leadership team support and monitor sheltered instruction implementation.

In their work with school principals, Alford and Niño (2011) affirmed,

> by embedding and sustaining teachers' professional development to build capacity to teach [ELs] effectively, a more authentic, in-depth understanding of the development that must take place at the classroom level and the embeddedness of curricular expectations and language development began to emerge. (p. 76)

How school leaders set up and sustain PL with a focus on ELs is ultimately tied to the vision and mission of the school.

What Would You Do?

As a school leader with a population of ELs, you have invested in a school-wide "strategies for teaching ELs" PL initiative. For the past 2 years, teachers have attended training during the district's PL days. Unfortunately, teachers are still struggling with implementation and monitoring academic growth of their ELs. Would you change the PL plan or stay with what you have in place? If you decide to change the plan, what first steps would you take?

_____

_____

_____

_____

This situation affirms the need for flexibility and informed decision-making. There are implications of going forward with a PL plan already in place just as there are for changing a PL plan. What is most important is the level of responsiveness to areas of need that may arise. Being prepared for honest feedback, revisions, and adjustments to PL plans is a necessary part of creating and sustaining highly effective learning communities.

Bringing It All Together

PL for all educators of ELs must be job embedded and long term. As the needs of the students we serve change, so must our PL efforts. The one-size-fits-all approach is leaving too many educators and their students out of the conversation.

As a component of linguistic equity, instructional expertise must highlight culturally responsive curriculum, pedagogy, and assessment. This reveals itself in our practice when we engage in PL that demands "that all students receive relevant and impactful instructional strategies and appropriately aligned tasks and assignments that allow them to practice and master content" (Fisher et al., 2020, p. 114); this is PL that results in equity. The last chapter of this book addresses the importance of communicating and establishing partnerships with families of linguistically diverse learners.

FOLLOW-UP QUESTIONS ....

1. Do you have a PL plan with a focus on ELs? What resources and/or data do you need to support your PL plan?

2. Who may need to collaborate with you to support your plan (e.g., finance officer, instructional coach, school leadership team)?

3. What are the short- and long-term goals of the PL plan as it relates to linguistically diverse learners?

4. What PL will be offered to support personnel? How might paraprofessionals, guidance counselors, and school attendance officers be included in short- and long-term PL plans?

5. What data points are being used (e.g., a staff needs assessment, student achievement data, staff requests for specific PL)?

6. If multiple PL plans are currently in place, how might they include linguistically diverse learners if they do not already? (How might those PL plans be supported and intersect? For example, does the writing instruction across the curriculum initiative align with the sheltered instruction PL? If not, how can you align them?)

7. How might differentiated PL support the students' greatest areas of need? How will those areas be evaluated through ongoing formal and informal assessments?

8. Is instructional coaching an option? If so, how might instructional coaches support teachers of ELs or be afforded PL specific to their needs?

9. What community partners might you consider that would support a school-wide customized PL plan?

10. How are PL outcomes being monitored and evaluated?

FURTHER GUIDANCE AND
SUPPORT RESOURCES ....

Organizations That Host Annual Conferences / Institutes

- ASCD (www.ascd.org/conferences.aspx)

- Center for Advanced Research on Language Acquisition (wida.wisc.edu)

- Center for Applied Linguistics (www.cal.org/what-we-do/institutes)

- ESEA Network (www.eseanetwork.org/conference)

- Pearson SIOP National Conference (getsupported.net/blog)

- National Association of Bilingual Education (www.nabe.org)

- National Association of Multicultural Education (nameorg.org)

- TESOL Calendar of Events (www.tesol.org/attend-and-learn/calendar-of -events)

- TESOL International Association (www.tesol.org)

- WestEd (www.wested.org/services/professional-development/ ?services=28552&single=yes)

- WIDA (wida.wisc.edu)

REFERENCES ....

Alford, B. J., & Niño, M. C. (2011). *Leading academic achievement for English language learners: A guide for principals.* Thousand Oaks, CA: Corwin Press.

Begay, B. (2018). Teaching the home language—Producing Diné speakers, establishing a Diné cultural identity. *Soleado Promising Practices from the Field.* Spring Edition.

Cooper, A. (2009). *Perceived efficacy level of elementary ESL teachers* (Doctoral dissertation). Retrieved from ProQuest LLC. (UMI No. 3355033)

Cooper, A. (2015). How is English language proficiency assessed under the Common Core Standards, and how can we use these data to inform and improve instruction? In G. Valdés, K. Menken, & M. Castro (Eds.), *Common Core, bilingual and English language learners: A resource for educators* (pp. 254–255). Philadelphia, PA: Caslon.

Curtis, A. (2008). The seven principles of professional development: From A to G. In *Leadership in English language teaching and learning* (pp. 117–127). Ann Arbor, MI: University of Michigan.

Darling-Hammond, L., Hyler, M. E., & Gardner, M. (2017). *Effective teacher.* Palo Alto, CA: Learning Policy Institute.

Dobrin, I. (2017, October 13). 'Get us out of here': Amid broken infrastructure, Puerto Ricans flee to Florida. *NPR*. Retrieved from https://www.npr.org/2017/10/13/557108484/-get-us-out-of-here-amid-broken-infrastructure-puerto-ricans-flee-to-florida

Fisher, D., Frey, N., Almarode, J., Flories, K., & Nagel, D. (2020). *PLC+: Better decisions and greater impact by design*. Thousand Oaks, CA: Corwin Press.

Guskey, T. R. (2000). *Evaluating professional development*. Thousand Oaks, CA: Corwin Press.

Honigsfeld, A., & Dove, M. (2012, February). Collaborative practices to support all students. *Principal Leadership. 12*, 40–44.

Jackson, H. (2016). *The 5 things instructional coaches must do, a manual*. Lexington, KY: Create Space Independent Platform.

Mizell, H. (2010). *Why professional development matters*. Oxford, OH: Learning Forward.

Soto-Hinman, I. (2010). ELL shadowing: Strengthening pedagogy and practice with pre-service and in-service teachers. *Research in Higher Education Journal, 8*, 1–11.

U.S. Department of Justice & U.S. Department of Education. (2015). *Dear colleague letter: English learner students and limited English proficient parents*. Retrieved from https://www2.ed.gov/about/offices/list/ocr/letters/colleague-el-201501.pdf

Zacarian, D. (2011). *Transforming schools for English learners: A comprehensive framework for school leaders*. Thousand Oaks, CA: Corwin Press.

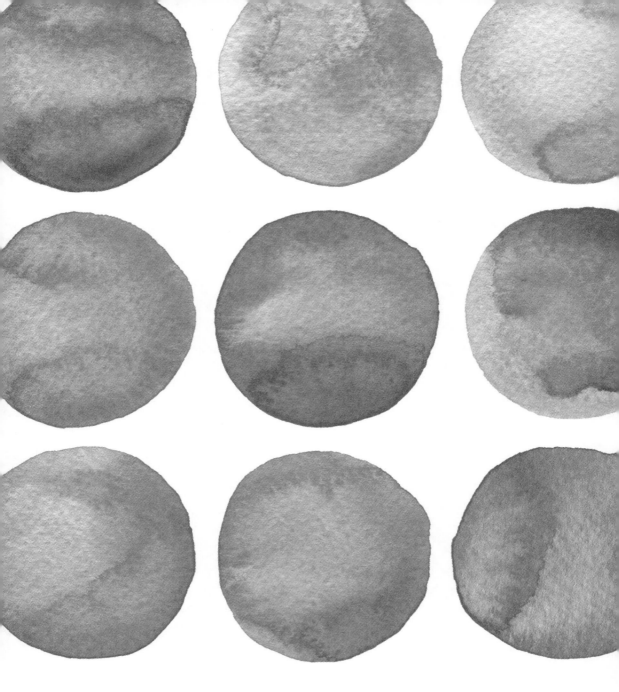

Us with them = All together

CHAPTER 5

Partnering With Parents of English Learners

Scenario: Helping Parents Analyze Their Child's English Language Proficiency Report

A school leader has worked extensively on improving communication with linguistically diverse families in his school. By working closely with interpreters, he has increased the number of families who attended school events in previous years. Parents and teachers are pleased with these outcomes, and the sense of "us vs. them" has diminished significantly. The school leadership team proposed inviting parents to a data analysis meeting with a focus on the assessments taken by their children. They also proposed that a portion of the meeting be dedicated to parents of English learners (ELs). With the help of translators, the team had training materials translated into multiple languages. They presented information about the annual English language assessment and included time for questions and answers. Childcare, interpreters, and light refreshments were available. Ultimately, the school leadership team and teachers wanted the families to have a better understanding of the assessments their children take and what the results mean. Legally, schools are required to send these results home, but by taking this extra step of having a meeting on campus to discuss the results, the school community has begun to establish a stronger relationship with linguistically diverse families. The data analysis meeting was well received and is now part of the school's annual meeting schedule.

This chapter explores how school leaders and teachers can foster stronger relationships with linguistically diverse families with the goal of ensuring positive outcomes for ELs. Historically, language as a barrier has been a focus and concern for both school communities and parents alike. It is no surprise that communication with families of ELs is one of the most common Civil Rights issues, as outlined in the "Dear Colleague Letter" (U.S. Department of Justice & U.S. Department of Education, 2015, p. 8). The historical underpinning of *Plyler v. Doe* (1982), a landmark court case that assured the rights of undocumented students to participate freely and to receive a free public school education in the United States, serves to remind us of the rights of the students we serve. Their participation in school unequivocally affords their parents the right to be informed and communicated with in a language they understand. In 2016, The U.S. Department of Education Office of English

Language Acquisition released the 10th chapter of the *English Learner Tool Kit*, which outlines the obligations that state education agencies (SEAs) and local education agencies (LEAs) have regarding communication with parents. Key points for the chapter include the following:

- SEAs and LEAs have an obligation to communicate meaningfully with limited English proficient (LEP) parents and to notify LEP parents adequately of information about any program, service, or activity called to the attention of non-LEP parents.

- LEAs must have a process to identify LEP parents and provide them with free and effective language assistance, such as translated materials or an appropriate and competent interpreter.

- Appropriate and competent translators or interpreters should have proficiency in target languages; ease of written and oral expression; knowledge of specialized terms or concepts; as well as be trained on their role, the ethics of interpreting and translating, and the need for confidentiality.

(U.S. Department of Education, 2016, p. 1)

As illustrated in the aforementioned scenario, fostering communication and partnerships with linguistically diverse families does not have to be a challenge; it can and should be an embedded practice for school communities. Mancilla and Blair (2019) call for parents and educators to form what they call a *language advocate alliance*. This alliance provides a lens for viewing advocacy for ELs and their families. Although a few definitions of EL advocacy exist, Mancilla's (2016) definition asserts an EL advocate is

a parent, guardian, close friend, or family member who speaks out or takes action on behalf of a child or family. An advocate is emotionally invested and driven by the goals and dreams they hold for the child or family, and/or they may be driven to advocate based on personal or family experiences of marginalization or discrimination within society and /or social institutions. (p. 120)

What stands out from this definition compared to earlier definitions is the emotional investment stipulation. Educators invest in students every day, but the level of their emotional investment is difficult to measure. Mancilla and Blair's (2019) research also found that parents of ELs want *more* information about their children's experiences in school. Parents are required by law to receive information about school components such as program models, curriculum, and instruction, but the parents interviewed wanted *more* information about these components (p. 105). While compliance requirements serve to provide important protections for children and their families, ask yourself: How can we move beyond compliance to a more proactive, collaborative framework that is informed by social justice?

Connecting Families and Community

Though some school communities have established EL family advisory committees and the like, those committees are not always as strongly connected to the school community as they should be. For example, one school I supported had both a PTA (parent–teacher association) and bilingual parent advisory council. Unfortunately, these committees did not work together! They had separate meetings, separate agendas, and separate committee members. Was this a modern-day example of separate but equal? Connecting EL families to school communities will take direct actions that are goal oriented. For example, are EL families members of your school's PTA? If not, how can school leaders not only encourage membership but also service to the board? If EL families are not aware of the vision, mission, and outcomes of such organizations, then expecting their involvement is unrealistic. EL families may need assistance in understanding the purpose of these organizations and ways to navigate being active members. Hernandez (2015) describes how a school leader mobilized his state-mandated EL advisory council committee by encouraging committee members to take leadership roles within and outside of the community (p. 95). This is an example of moving beyond establishing committees with EL families for compliance purposes to actively engaging family members as advocates for ELs. The goal is to embed such groups in the school community while respecting EL families, funds of knowledge, and power to better serve their children and the school community as a whole.

Another example would be helping EL families connect to community organizations, such as social service agencies that offer assistance with childcare, clothing, food, employment, healthcare, and the like. As an English as a second language (ESL) teacher, I remember my students receiving dental care through my school's mobile dentist partnership. I also remember one of my schools having a girl scout troop on campus that met after school. Some school leaders have hosted job fairs at their schools. By inviting community service groups to meet with families on campus, it can reduce the need for parents, especially EL families, to try and navigate those agencies in isolation.

Parent Communication Preferences

Surveying parents about how they want to be communicated with is one of the first steps to strengthening EL family–school partnerships. Similar to the professional learning needs assessment presented in Chapter 4, a parent communication preference survey can be used to inform how and why a school leader communicates with linguistically diverse families. Often, English language documents are shared with parents through a student's backpack and/or are posted on a school website. If the school houses a significant population of students who speak a particular language besides

English, it behooves educators to translate important documents into that language. Admittedly, it may strike some readers as onerous to be called upon to translate every document—especially for less commonly represented languages—but no one could possibly argue against the need to ensure clear communication with families. Regardless of the number of speakers of a particular language, principals and teachers have the responsibility to assure that all students and their families have all information made available to them.

Let's assume multiple languages are represented within a school community. How might a school leader decide how best to use data about languages spoken within a school so that as many families as possible are being reached?

The school language profile in Figure 5.1 shows the languages represented at one school. By administering a parent communication preference survey, school leaders will be able to make better informed decisions related to communication needs and use the preferred method of communication for all families. In addition to sending notices home through the students' backpacks, more personalized ways of communicating can be offered. For example, if a significant number of Spanish-speaking families prefer to receive school messages via text messaging, then the school leader could invest in an electronic messaging system, such as FASTalk (which offers, among other features, translated text messages between parents and teachers). This option

Figure 5.1 Sample School Language Profile

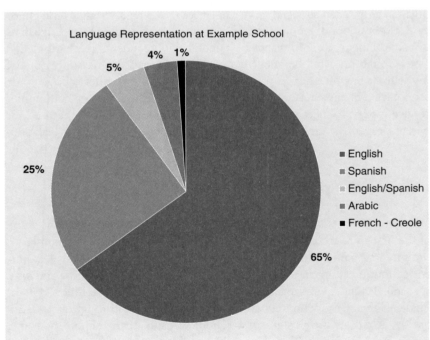

Figure 5.2 Sample Translation

English	Arabic
In addition to notices sent home and posted on the school website, how would you like to receive notifications from the school? Please select one.	بالإضافة إلى الإشعارات التي تم إرسالها إلى عنوان سكنكم ونشرها على موقع المدرسة على الويب، ما هي وسية التواصل الأخرى التي تود استلام إشعارات المدرسة عن طريقها؟ يُرجى اختيار وسيلة تواصل واحدة.
1. Text messages √	1. رسالة نصية √
2. Email	2. رسالة بريد إلكتروني
3. Recorded voice mail message	3. رسالة صوتية مسجلة عبر البريد
4. None of these	4. لا أرغب في أي من هذه الوسائل

is also beneficial for the languages spoken by smaller populations of families, such as Arabic in Figure 5.2. In addition to how parents prefer to receive information, it is imperative—and it is the law—that all languages represented within a school community have access to documents in a language they can understand.

Every Student Succeeds Act (2015) guidance requires school districts to keep parents and guardians of ELs informed of their rights. They must be provided with opportunities to be involved in their children's education, including having access to information about the following:

- registration and enrollment in school and school programs
- grievance procedures and notices of nondiscrimination
- language assistance programs
- parent handbooks
- report cards
- gifted and talented programs
- student discipline policies and procedures
- magnet and charter schools
- special education and related services, and meetings to discuss special education

- parent–teacher conferences

- requests for parent permission for student participation in school activities

An evaluation of how and to what extent each of the aforementioned areas are being communicated with EL families could provide a school leader with insight about his or her school community and could help the leader make informed decisions about what further information should be sent to families.

Helping EL Families Understand the Academic Calendar

Don't assume that linguistically diverse families will automatically have a clear understanding of the school calendar and attendance policies. Families new to U.S. schools may not be able to initially interpret school procedures, climate, and culture—attributes that may be quite different from those of their home countries. Chronic absenteeism and transportation barriers may be a factor for some ELs, as with all students, but before we even begin to consider their causes, we must first understand how attendance mandates and school calendars are communicated.

Begin by critically examining your own assumptions about EL families. When we are stuck in compliance mode, we often think of our families as "file folders"—passive recipients to fill up with notices, rather than as our partners in their child's educational career. Most school calendars are available to students and their families as notices and on the district website. Are the calendars available in multiple languages? Figure 5.3 shows one district's website, which offers the downloadable calendar in multiple languages. Figure 5.4 shows samples of the calendar in two different languages.

Figure 5.3 Downloadable School Calendar in Multiple Languages

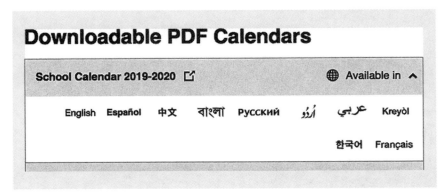

Figure 5.4 Sample School Calendar in English and Haitian Creole

School Calendar 2019-2020	
Sept 5	FIRST DAY OF SCHOOL FOR ALL STUDENTS (Partial school day for pre-kindergarten public school students)
Sept 12	Parent Teacher Conferences for Elementary Schools and K–8 Schools (Evening)*
Sept 19	Parent Teacher Conferences for Middle Schools (Evening)*
Sept 26	Parent Teacher Conferences for High Schools, K–12, and 6–12 Schools (Evening)*
Sept 30-Oct 1	Rosh Hashanah (Schools closed)
Oct 9	Yom Kippur (Schools closed)
Oct 14	Columbus Day (Schools closed)
Nov 5	Election Day/Chancellor's Conference Day for Staff Development (Students do not attend school)
Nov 6-7	Parent Teacher Conferences for Middle Schools and District 75 Programs (Evening and Afternoon)*
Nov 11	Veterans Day Observed (Schools closed)
Kalandriye Lekòl 2019-2020	
5 septanm	PREMYE JOU LEKÒL POU TOUT ELÈV (Demi jounen pou elèv pre-k ki nan lekòl leta yo)
12 septanm	Konferans Pwofesè-Paran Pou Lekòl Primè Ak Lekòl Klas K–8yèm Ane yo (Aswè)*
19 septanm	Konferans Pwofesè-Paran Pou Lekòl Presegondè yo (Aswè)*
26 septanm	Konferans Pwofesè-Paran Pou Lekòl Segondè yo, Klas K–12yèm Ane yo ak 6yèm-12yèm Ane yo (Aswè)*
30 septamn - 1ye oktòb	Rosh Hashanah (Pa gen lekòl)
9 oktòb	Yom Kippur (Pa gen lekòl)
14 oktòb	Columbus Day (Pa gen lekòl)
5 novanm	Jounen Eleksyon/Jounen Konferans Chanselye Pou Fòmasyon Anplwaye (Elèv yo pa gen pou al lekòl jou sa)
6-7 novanm	Konferans Pwofesè-Paran Pou Lekòl Presegondè Ak Pwogram Distri 75 yo (Aswè Ak Apremidi)*
11 novanm	Fèt Veteran (Pa gen lekòl)

Because the district/school calendar is such an integral centerpiece of the workings of schools, in addition to providing the calendars in the relevant languages, we also want to do everything possible to ensure that parents know the meaning of key phrases, such as the following:

- Registration begins/ends
- First day of school
- Teacher professional learning day
- Early release
- Parent/teacher conferences
- End of marking term
- Report cards sent home
- Holiday—Winter break
- Graduation
- Last day of school
- Summer school

Such phrases, without accurate translation and interpretation, could potentially be problematic for EL families. Take the phrases "early release" or "teacher professional learning" for example, and think about how you would explain these to a family who speaks another language besides English.

Scenario: Early Release/Late Pick-Up

An elementary school assistant principal described an experience where a kindergarten EL had to be returned to school by the bus driver when no one was home on an early release day to receive the child. The family was living in a temporary housing situation; technically, they were considered homeless. The family members listed as approved to be contacted on the registration form could not leave work to pick up the child. Eventually, another relative was contacted and had to go through the required steps to secure the parent's permission to pick up the child from school. Several hours went by before the child was picked up from school. What started out as an early release day turned out to be a long, slightly traumatic day for the student and her family members.

How could that situation have been avoided? What support or reminders did the family need in their native language to avoid this situation? What could the school leaders have done before the early release day to notify or remind students and their families?

We can't always take for granted that family members will comprehend the meaning of the language used in our calendars. Helping EL families understand the school calendar ensures they have access to information they need to best support their child. One school, with a significant population of EL families, offered a session about the school calendar as part of their open house events before the school year started. Making this important information available in multiple languages—and taking the extra steps to ensure it is understood—is not only helpful but necessary.

Grade Level Placements of ELs and What Parents Need to Know

The manner in which ELs are registered and placed into grade levels and classes is relatively similar to the process for general education students, depending upon language support programs offered by the district. The matriculation process, however, can be challenging for linguistically diverse parents and their children. Parents are often surprised to learn that each SEA and LEA in the United States has the authority to set its own graduation requirements, which means that grade level placement varies depending on the SEA or LEA of enrollment. Often, parents expect that their children will be placed in the grade parallel to the student's native-English-speaking peers;

however, with seat time requirements, coursework disparities, and the students' level of English proficiency, it is quite likely that an EL will require additional classes in order to graduate from high school within 4 years—depending on when they arrived in the United States. This can be especially discouraging when students arrive in the United States as secondary students and are performing academically below grade level.

At the secondary level, we also must take into account whether students have completed coursework in their home countries or another country. By conducting a thorough evaluation of secondary (foreign) transcripts, we can determine whether students may receive credit for the courses they completed abroad. Without a transcript evaluation, educators may unintentionally penalize students who are entitled to such credits by placing them further back on their educational journey than necessary. Bear in mind that because ELs are at greater risk of dropping out of high school than their native-English-speaking peers, we have an obligation to grant them as much credit as possible for the coursework they have completed.

> School districts have become proactive in educating incoming parents about the state laws, local board of education policies, and operating procedures which govern how grade level placement is determined. Part of my job as a Guidance Counselor who specializes in supporting ELs and their families in an urban school district outside of metro Atlanta, GA is to conduct one-on-one parent conferences with each high school student and his or her family members during the initial enrollment process. During these individualized meetings, families are provided with local graduation requirements, a review of their foreign transcript evaluation, an explanation of the student's grade level placement, and a recommended class schedule that reflects the student's college and career goals. By participating in individualized parent learning opportunities, parents can navigate a new educational system and make informed decisions about their child's educational career. **P. Grant, Guidance Counselor and Foreign Transcript Evaluator (Personal Communication, April 22, 2019)**

Guidance Counselor P. Grant explains the importance of an efficient enrollment process that considers parents as partners, not passive recipients of sterile information. It is important for school leaders to have materials translated into multiple languages and to have the contact information of a district representative who can answer additional questions. Grade level placements may be partly decided by central office representatives. Most likely, though, the school leader (who may delegate the responsibility to a guidance counselor and/or lead ESL teacher) is responsible for following through with the grade level placement instructions.

Granting credit from prior schooling to ELs is a great example of a policy that promotes access and equity. Callahan and Shifrer (2016) researched course-taking patterns by ELs in secondary schools, and their findings suggested

Table 5.1   High School Transcript, Korean to English Translation

First Semester	
Subject	**Units**
Korean Language 1	4
Korean Language 2	4
Mathematics 1	4
Mathematics 2	2
English 1	3
Practical English 1	2
Social Students	2
Korean History	3
Life & Ethics	2
Science	3
Physical Education	2
Music & Life	2
Art Creation	2
Technology & Home Economics	2
Total Units	**37**

school leaders should evaluate their approaches to course placement for ELs. This suggestion is based on the finding that, despite the focus on the overall academic achievement of ELs, ELs remain blocked from access to a large proportion of the core curriculum, electives, and advanced placement classes because they are locked into English language development and/or intervention classes (Callahan, 2005; National Academies of Sciences, Engineering, and Medicine, 2017). The transcript sample in Table 5.1 shows that a 10th grade student from South Korea has completed a number of courses. If this student enrolled in your district with this translated transcript, what courses would he be enrolled in? How would you communicate to his parents his course assignment process and the courses he would be enrolled into? Teachers in your school would also need to know about this student's prior school experiences in order to think about the types of supports the student might need.

Bullying

There has been a nationwide interest and increase in antibullying campaigns in school settings. In a survey conducted by the Southern Poverty Law Center

(Costello, 2016) of 10,000 teachers, counselors, administrators, and other personnel who worked in schools, ninety percent of participants reported the 2016 presidential election had a negative impact on schools. They reported an upswing in verbal harassment; the use of slurs and derogatory language; and disturbing incidents involving swastikas, Nazi salutes, and Confederate flags (Costello, 2016, p. 4). Some of the survey results included the following:

- Eight in 10 reported heightened anxiety on the part of marginalized students, including immigrants, Muslims, African Americans, and LGBT (lesbian, gay, bisexual, and transgender) students.

- Four in 10 had heard derogatory language directed at students of color, Muslims, immigrants, and people based on gender or sexual orientation.

- Although two-thirds reported that administrators had been "responsive," four out of 10 didn't think their schools had action plans to respond to incidents of hate and bias.

(Costello, 2016, p. 4)

There is no doubt about the negative impact bullying can have on a child both short and long term. All parties—the student bullying, the student being bullied, and those witnessing the acts of bullying—are negatively affected. If a child who is experiencing bullying in school is an EL, imagine how difficult it would be to communicate these experiences to a parent, sibling, or teacher. The U.S. Department of Health and Human Services maintains a website, stopbullying.gov, dedicated to eliminating bullying. This website defines bullying as unwanted aggressive behavior, observed or perceived power imbalance, or repetition of behaviors or high likelihood of repetition (U.S. Department of Health and Human Services, n.d.). However, bullying can be complex, and defining it in a useful way can also be complex (see Table 5.2 for types of bullying).

Keeping language and cultural differences in mind, articulating these complexities and explaining how school leaders can support EL families who might experience bullying is important for creating and sustaining positive partnerships.

Following is a situation where an EL in elementary school was a victim of direct bullying. As you read the scenario, think about the series of events and whether the issue was resolved favorably. If this happened in your school, would the outcome be similar or different?

Scenario: Bullying in Elementary School

Li Min, her husband, and their daughter are originally from China. Their daughter is in fourth grade and has been attending the local elementary

Table 5.2 Types of Bullying

Type of Bullying	Description	Example
Direct	Student targeted in person	Amed, a middle school student, is called racial slurs daily at the bus stop by older students. He doesn't report it in fear of additional harassment.
Indirect	Student targeted through nondirect communication	Photos of Amed changing into gym clothes are sent around to his peers via text message. Other students know who took and sent out the photos. They show Amed the photos on their phones. He is angry and humiliated. Still, he does not report it due to fear and embarrassment.
Physical, verbal, relational	Student physically assaulted, threatened with assault, students in a dating and/or obsessive relationship	The perpetrator hears that Amed is angry about the text messages and confronts him in the hallway. A physical altercation occurs; Amed defends himself. Both students are suspended from school for 3 days due to fighting in school. Amed's parents are called and a notice is sent home in English explaining the suspension. Amed doesn't want his parents to worry and assures them he is being a good student.
Damage to property	Personal belongings stolen or destroyed	Amed's cell phone was taken from him, thrown, and stepped on during the altercation. The screen is cracked and is not powering on correctly.

school for 1 year. Over the past few months, Li Min's daughter has been bullied by her peers. She regularly comes home crying because other students make fun of her accent and Asian background. Li Min is not sure how to best help her daughter. She does not feel it would be appropriate to speak to the teacher or principal because of their level of authority. Furthermore, even if she wanted to talk to someone at the school, there would be no way to communicate because she does not speak English. Once, Li Min tried going into the school's front office and the secretary shouted at her and gave her a frustrated look, and so she left. Li Min also struggles to understand American culture, and this has contributed to a lack of trust.

She and her husband start to think about moving their daughter to a new school, which would require moving to a new neighborhood. They begin to believe that this is the only potential solution. Before taking this drastic step, Li Min decides to ask a few of her Chinese American friends on WeChat, a group messaging and social media platform, what she should do. A couple of the moms on the app have been in the United States longer and understand the school system better than Li Min. They tell her that she has the right to ask for an interpreter any time she needs one at the school! They also tell her that she definitely needs to visit the school and talk with the teacher and principal—they tell her "that's how Americans solve this bullying problem." Li Min is worried about the implications of visiting the school and whether it will affect how her daughter's teacher treats her, but she decides to trust her friends. With their help, she sets up a meeting at the school and asks that an interpreter be present.

As the school leader, think about how you would respond to this family's request to meet with you and/or the child's teacher. Here are some questions to consider:

- What would you do to prepare for the meeting?

- What would you do to prepare the interpreter?

- Have there been other incidents of bullying in that grade level or is this an isolated incident?

- What might your next steps be after the meeting?

- Keeping the language difference in mind, would you handle this situation slightly differently or the same if the family were native English speakers?

- What language and supports would Li Min (or Amed, from Table 5.2) need in order to fully be able to articulate what happened to them?

Does your school have an antibullying policy? How are instances of bullying typically handled? Be proactive whenever you can, and be reactive when you must be. One proactive step—one that may have helped prevent a situation like Li Min's from escalating as far as it did—is making sure your school's antibullying policy is readily available and translated into different languages. In reacting to this situation, it's important to recognize that the secretary's response to Li Min was a form of bullying in itself (a perceived power imbalance resulting in aggressive behavior) and was unacceptable. Although the exchange could be interpreted as frustrating for both parties, once Li Min left, she had yet another reason to not trust the school personnel. What follow-up conversation would you have with the secretary? What type of training would she and other staff members need in order to engage positively with all families, especially EL families?

Supporting Your Staff to Build Positive Relationships With EL Families

Assumptions About EL Families

Schools have historically underestimated and underutilized ELs' parents' ability and willingness to assist in their children's academic success. Educators who wish to create successful partnerships with EL families must learn to reflect on their own biases and assumptions, which can be uncomfortable.

However, negative thinking and comments about EL families are disparaging and can be simply untrue. Consider the following comments:

- *They don't value education*
- *They should speak English—they are in the United States now*
- *They are poor*
- *They are uneducated/illiterate*
- *They should go back to their country*
- *They are taking jobs from Americans*

Have you heard comments like these in a school setting? If so, what did you do? The answer may depend upon where and who you are as an educator. For those more comfortable confronting deficit thinking, they might ask their colleague why they think that way or what evidence they have in making such a statement. Others may not do anything but walk away, feeling uneasy and uncomfortable with what they heard. Gorski's (2019) work around confronting racial bias is forthright:

> Racial equity cannot be achieved with an obsessive commitment to "meeting people where they are" when "where they are" is fraught with racial bias and privilege. Students, families, and educators experiencing racism cannot afford to wait for us to saunter toward a more serious racial equity vision. (Gorski, 2019, p. 19)

It would be important to address commons like this when they are heard if possible. If not, following up with the person who made the comments privately could also be an approach. For school leaders, setting the tone for antiracist practices, respect for diversity, and active inclusivity…

Addressing negative biases like these is the foundation for building positive relationships with EL families.

Customized Professional Learning

As expressed throughout this book, custom-designed professional learning is needed for the learning to be authentic and proactive. We clearly need to move beyond the "bring a dish from your culture" and other one-and-done school "diversity" events. Consider the research conducted by Moll, Amanti, Neff, and Gonzalez (1992) that positioned teachers as researchers as a way to understand funds of knowledge as it relates to teaching. Their research broadened the understanding of culture so that it went beyond "folkloric displays, such as storytelling, arts, crafts, and dance performance" (p. 139). Instead, educators can act upon the importance of "strategic knowledge and related activities essential in households' functioning, development, and well-being" (Moll et al., 1992, p. 139). Professional learning has to dig deeper to be effective, and that begins with strong relationships between the educators and their EL families.

Professional learning around how to build and sustain relationships with EL families can be multilayered and must be context specific. A good place to begin is with your professional learning needs assessment (see Chapter 4) and any data about staff needs related to communicating with families that may have been revealed. If the assessment doesn't ask the kinds of questions that would provide useful information about this topic, think about what questions you can add that would be helpful, such as

- To what extent do I know what I need to know about my students and their families?

- Is the student and his or her family bilingual and biliterate? Is the family interested in receiving information about social service agencies in our community?

- Is there a family member who is interested in serving in a leadership capacity within a school-sponsored event and/or organization (e.g., PTA, career day, media center committee, curriculum adoption)?

Unlike implementing a new teaching strategy, being prepared for all of the possible ways to communicate with and partner with EL families is nearly impossible. One precursor to this work is to assure that educators are being nonjudgmental and unbiased about the families they serve, because biases can taint communication, breed resentment, and impede connection. Here are a few examples of educator biases that would be obstacles to open and productive communication:

- Assuming parents of ELs do not care about their child's education because they do not approach you about their child's academic performance.

- Assuming EL families have the same experiences if they come from the same countries.

- Assuming all ELs are low income.

- Changing ELs' names to a nickname or a more American-sounding name because they are perceived as difficult to pronounce.

- Telling EL families to speak English at home.

- Not recognizing various academic strengths because they don't fit the "expectation" of an EL.

- Assuming EL families are not literate in their native language.

These examples are representations of teachers being, perhaps unintentionally, biased about linguistically diverse students and their families, or ignorant of a difference in cultural norms. Have you ever witnessed any of these behaviors? Besides the school leader, many individuals come into contact with EL families: front office staff, classroom teachers, bus drivers, school nurses, social workers, guidance counselors, and paraprofessionals. Think holistically about how those team members are educated about EL families. TESOL International Association (2019) recently released The 6 Principles® Quick Guide for Paraeducators. As part of The 6 Principles series, they created a resource for paraeducators to learn more about ELs and the supports they need in the classroom. This is an example of a direct approach to supporting paraeducators who work directly with ELs on a regular basis but often receive little, or no, professional learning on EL needs. Any effort to include ancillary staff members as part of the work of building partnerships with EL families is extremely beneficial to your school community both short and long term. This is especially important because federal policy requires LEAs to allot a portion of their Title I funding to family engagement programs.

Providing Translation Services

One way to ensure accurate direct communication with EL families is to utilize professional interpreters—and training your staff to use them appropriately and effectively. One school leader embedded professional learning for his staff with a focus on using interpreters during parent teacher conferences. The elementary school is in an urban setting and is considered a Title I school. Over 85% of the students are identified as EL and multiple languages are spoken by the student population. Although the school's professional learning had focused heavily on instructional practices in the past, they had not specifically focused on how to effectively communicate with the use of interpreters. The new training was embedded in their year-long professional learning plan and included all staff members, including the interpreters. The school has successfully implemented monthly parent meetings with interpreters.

Following are some suggestions for working with an interpreter:

- If possible, meet with the interpreter prior to the meeting with the parents. This allows for introductions and setting the context for the meeting, or what will be the focus of discussion (e.g., report cards, preparing for an individual education plan meeting).

- Speak directly to the parent, not the interpreter. Avoid saying "tell them…"

- Create a balanced seating arrangement; avoid sitting behind your desk with the parent and interpret on the opposite side. Arrange desks so they are in a semicircle or sit around a table.

- Speak slowly but not loudly.

- Use short phrases and avoid the use of acronyms, educational jargon, or other language that may not be interpretable.

- Allow time for the parents and the interpreter to ask questions.

- Pause so the interpreter can interpret.

- Be patient.

Source: List particularly adapted from the Refugee Health Technical Assistance Center, 2011

(List particularly adapted from the Refugee Health Technical Assistance Center, 2011)

Supporting your staff with professional learning needs that focus on EL families is a social justice issue. Solving the equation "us with them = all together" is imperative if schools are to truly provide access and become more equitable for culturally and linguistically diverse students and their families. Preparing and embedding supports for those who impact student achievement is an investment in them and the students they serve.

What Would You Do?: The Decision

In Chapter 1, we considered a request from Mr. and Mrs. Suarez to move their first-grade child from the bilingual class into a general education class. They were concerned that their son was not progressing in his English reading skills; his English proficiency was intermediate, and he had been retained in the first grade.

After meeting with and listening to the concerns of Mr. and Mrs. Suarez, the principal met with the bilingual education teacher for her input. The teacher indicated that the student was making progress and was one of the higher performing students in the class. The teacher felt the student was not being challenged as much as he could be and agreed with the parents: He should be moved to a general education first-grade class. The principal invited the general education first-grade teacher to meet with the student and the bilingual education teacher. The child was transitioned into a general education class with a segment of ESL support each day. His parents were informed that their request was granted and were regularly kept abreast of his progress. They were pleased their child was doing well in his new class.

_____

_____

_____

_____

In this case, the school leader obliged with the parents' wishes to have their son moved from the bilingual program to a general education class. Some may not agree with this decision, but we must keep what is best for the students, as communicated by their parents, at the center of any decision. Ultimately, we all want ELs to be as successful as possible. We also want parents to become strong, trusting partners with us on this journey toward academic success. We can do that by being proactive in our efforts to create inclusive and equitable schools with ELs and their families.

Bringing It All Together

This chapter affirmed the importance of principals fostering relationships with linguistically diverse families—not only because it is the right thing to do but also because it is a core principle of creating and sustaining equitable schools. We cannot afford to isolate or further marginalize families from culturally and linguistically diverse backgrounds if we are responsible for educating their children. The scenarios and questions posed in this chapter were strategically selected to offer real-life example of the experiences of EL students and their families.

FOLLOW-UP QUESTIONS ....

1. Is communicating with linguistically diverse parents an area in need of improvement for your school community? If so, how do you know?

2. What are the procedures and processes for having documents translated into other languages besides English?

3. What process is in place to assure interpreters are available for parent meetings?

4. What happens when parents who do not speak English arrive at your school without a meeting but need help or have a concern?

5. Who on staff is a trained interpreter? If there are none, how do you request interpreters when needed? In your school, has any professional learning been offered with a focus on communication with diverse families?

   a. If not, what might those sessions include? Which community partners might support these sessions?

   b. If so, what follow-up sessions are planned?

6. What stakeholders (e.g., PTA, community organizations) are involved with supporting school initiatives? Do those organizations have culturally and linguistically diverse representation, specifically from EL families?

7. What opportunities and/or invitations can be offered to EL families who are interested in being more involved? How and where are those opportunities advertised?

8. Do you have, or could you create, a language advocate alliance within your school community? If so, who might your allies be? What obstacles might you anticipate? How can you overcome those obstacles?

9. What additional steps will you take to create and sustain partnerships with EL families?

FURTHER GUIDANCE AND SUPPORT RESOURCES ....

Additional Readings

- TESOL Community & Family Toolkit (www.tesol.org/docs/default-source /advocacy/tesol-community-and-family-toolkit.pdf? sfvrsn=121fe6dc_0)

- UnidosUs Progress Report K–12 Education (progressreport.co/back2 school)

- U.S. Department of Education, Office of English Language Acquisition Family Tool Kit (ncela.ed.gov/family-toolkit)

- WIDA Family Engagement (wida.wisc.edu/teach/learners/engagement)

Blog

- Immigrant Connections blog (www.immigrantsrefugeesandschools.org /blog)

Organizations

- Open Doors for Multicultural Families (www.multiculturalfamilies.org /programs-services)

- National PTA (www.pta.org/home/events/event-list)

Webinar

- White House Task Force on New Americans Educational and Linguistic Integration

- Webinar Series (www2.ed.gov/about/offices/list/oela/webinars/new -americans/index.html)

Websites

- Bridging Refugee Youth & Children Services (brycs.org)

- Colorín Colorado For Families (www.colorincolorado.org/families)

- Immigrant Connections (www.immigrantsrefugeesandschools.org)

REFERENCES ....

Callahan, R. M. (2005). Tracking and high school English learners: Limiting opportunity to learn. *American Educational Research Journal, 42*(2), 305–328.

Callahan, R. M., & Shifrer, D. (2016). Equitable access for secondary English learner students. *Educational Administration Quarterly, 52*(3), 463–496. doi:10.1177/0013161x16648190

Costello, M. B. (2016). *After election day: The Trump effect: The impact of the 2016 presidential election on our nation's schools.* Montgomery, AL: Southern Poverty Law Center.

Every Student Succeeds Act of 2015, Pub. L. 114–95, §1177 (2015)

Gorski, P. (2019, April). Avoiding racial equity detours. *Educational Leadership. 76*, 56–61.

Hernandez, S. (2015). In what ways can school policies limit authentic involvement of English language learners'/emergent bilinguals' parents, and how can this be addressed? In G. Valdéz, K. Menken, & M. Castro (Eds.), *Common Core bilingual and English language learners: A resource for educators* (pp. 95–96). Philadelphia, PA: Caslon.

Mancilla, L. (2016). *La voz y presencia de padres Latinos: Understanding family engagement practices that support the language education of K–12 Latino emergent bilinguals* (Doctoral dissertation). Retrieved from ProQuest Dissertation and Thesis. (Accession Order No. 10251842)

Mancilla, L., & Blair, A. (2019). Language advocate alliances. In H. Lineville & J. Whiting (Eds.), *Advocacy in English language teaching and learning* (pp. 98–109). New York, NY: Routledge.

Moll, L. C., Amanti, C., Neff, D., & Gonzalez, N. (1992). Funds of knowledge for teaching: Using a qualitative approach to connect homes and classrooms. *Theory Into Practice, 31*(2), 132–141. doi:10.1080/00405849209543534

National Academies of Sciences, Engineering, and Medicine. (2017). *Promoting the educational success of children and youth learning English: Promising futures.* Washington, DC: The National Academies Press. doi:10.17226/24677

Plyler v. Doe, 457 U.S. 202 (1982)

Refugee Health Technical Assistance Center. (2011). *Best practices for communicating through an interpreter.* Retrieved from https://refugeehealthta.org /access-to-care/language-access/best-practices-communicating-through-an -interpreter/

TESOL International Association. (2019). *The 6 Principles quick guide for paraeducators.* Alexandria, VA: TESOL Press.

U.S. Department of Education. (2016). *Chapter 10: Tools and resources for ensuring meaningful communication with limited English proficient parents.* Retrieved from https://www2.ed.gov/about/offices/list/oela/english-learner-toolkit/chap10.pdf

U.S. Department of Health and Human Services. (n.d.). What is bullying. Retrieved from https://www.stopbullying.gov/bullying/what-is-bullying

U.S. Department of Justice & U.S. Department of Education. (2015). *Dear colleague letter: English learner students and limited English proficient parents.* Retrieved from https://www2.ed.gov/about/offices/list/ocr/letters/colleague-el-201501.pdf

Afterword

I remember when I heard the first mention of a deadly virus spreading throughout the world. It was early one November morning in 2019. My husband, always concerned about my travel schedule, told me about an article he had just read. I assured him I wasn't going out of the country anytime soon, but, I have to admit, the news article he showed me about it was scary. Jump ahead a few months, and the reality of COVID-19, a new virus that easily spreads through person-to-person contact had reached the United States. By March 2020, schools and businesses were making plans to close. The academic school year as we knew it had come to an abrupt halt. Citizens were told to "shelter in place" and to adhere to "social distancing" guidelines—terms that were new to us but would soon become ubiquitous in the news and in our lives. Life as we knew it had changed. What did this mean for the millions of school children? Within a short time, distance learning became a necessity. In various forms, online learning, homeschooling, virtual learning, and the like became the primary modes of instruction. One question kept arising from concerned colleagues: "What about English learners?"

It was—and is—an important question; it's the question we're asking throughout this book. Aside from impacting our social-emotional health, COVID-19 elevated the stark disparities among various K–12 learning populations across the United States: disparities such as students from low-income households, those deemed "at-risk," those living in food deserts, those experiencing homelessness, and students who lacked access to healthcare. Now added to this list were those on the other side of the "digital divide," or those who did not have access to the internet and portal learning devices. All of these disparities were already in existence, but before the COVID-19 pandemic, they did not strike panic and imbue in people a true sense of urgency for our most vulnerable learners.

So…what *about* English learners? The first part of my answer to that question is this: English learners and their families are resilient. As with other life challenges, some of which were described in this book, English learner families can and have overcome. Schools and programs that did not have plans in place for English learners prior to the COVID-19 pandemic will face an especially difficult, yet not impossible, challenge in putting plans in place now. Here's what we can do when it comes to living and learning when a catastrophe strikes.

Value Human Connection

What is important to keep in mind and act upon is the need to keep the human connection strong—the connection between schools and the students they serve. This is important because social distancing mandates insist on distance, all but eliminating the social aspect of schooling. Despite not seeing and being with our students in physical classrooms, our kind words of encouragement can go a long way. Through email, phone calls, and handwritten notes, we can stay connected to our learning communities.

Advocate Alongside

As the field develops and offers resources for English learner families, we can continue to serve as advocates. Helping families have access to learning opportunities as well as health and wellness resources is imperative. A number of school communities have offered meals to families in need. Books and packets of learning materials have been delivered to families who do not have access to the internet or personal learning devices. Sharing information is part of advocacy, but so is helping families advocate for themselves. Do your English learner families know how to contact school officials or their children's teachers when schools move from a traditional model to a virtual one? Do they know the expectation for continuation—or discontinuation—of services during this time? If not, how can those who may be more adept at navigating spaces during the shutdown help these families navigate those spaces as well?

Continue to Acknowledge Student Strengths

As a result of schools shutting down or moving online, a number of discussions have arisen around students' academic performance declining and the achievement gap widening. I'd like to suggest a more asset-based lens to assess the impact of COVID-19 or any other disaster that interrupts normal routines. First, as with any assessment, we need data to make assertions (rather than assumptions) about student academic performance. That data should be interpreted in a way that acknowledges the skills and knowledge that students have maintained *and* gained while their schools were closed or virtual. How can we celebrate their gains and growth in a way that can aid in supporting any areas that were not as developed? How can we include student voices as a part of those conversations? How have students adjusted to more autonomous learning? How has this experience strengthened them and their awareness of how homes, schools, and broader communities work together to keep each other as safe and healthy as possible?

It is my hope that this book has served as a useful resource for you. I hope that you can now begin to or continue the work you are doing for English learners within your learning communities and beyond. I hope that you are more prepared to create and sustain, whether in a traditional format or a virtual one, an equitable and inclusive learning environment for English learners.

Index

A SAGE Publishing Company

Helping educators make the greatest impact

CORWIN HAS ONE MISSION: to enhance education through intentional professional learning.

We build long-term relationships with our authors, educators, clients, and associations who partner with us to develop and continuously improve the best evidence-based practices that establish and support lifelong learning.

Solutions YOU WANT | Experts YOU TRUST | Results YOU NEED

EVENTS

>>> **INSTITUTES**

Corwin Institutes provide large regional events where educators collaborate with peers and learn from industry experts. Prepare to be recharged and motivated!

corwin.com/institutes

ON-SITE PD

>>> **ON-SITE PROFESSIONAL LEARNING**

Corwin on-site PD is delivered through high-energy keynotes, practical workshops, and custom coaching services designed to support knowledge development and implementation.

corwin.com/pd

>>> **PROFESSIONAL DEVELOPMENT RESOURCE CENTER**

The PD Resource Center provides school and district PD facilitators with the tools and resources needed to deliver effective PD.

corwin.com/pdrc

ONLINE

>>> **ADVANCE**

Designed for K–12 teachers, Advance offers a range of online learning options that can qualify for graduate-level credit and apply toward license renewal.

corwin.com/advance

Contact a PD Advisor at (800) 831-6640 or visit www.corwin.com for more information